POPULAR ENGLISH IDIOMS AND PHRASES

ENGLISH IDIOMATIC EXPRESSIONS

MANIK JOSHI

Dedication

THIS BOOK IS
DEDICATED
TO THOSE
WHO REALIZE
THE POWER OF ENGLISH
AND WANT TO
LEARN IT
SINCERELY

Copyright Notice

All rights reserved. Please note that the content in this book is protected under copyright law. This book is for your personal use only. No part of this book may be reproduced, stored in a retrieval system, or transmitted, in any form or by any means, electronic, mechanical, recording, or otherwise, without the prior written permission of the author.

Copyright Holder -- Manik Joshi
License -- Standard Copyright License
Year of Publication -- 2014
Email -- manik85joshi@gmail.com

****

IMPORTANT NOTE

This Book is Part of a Series
SERIES Name: "English Daily Use"
[A Forty-Book Series]
BOOK Number: 28
BOOK Title: "Popular English Idioms and Phrases"
****

Table of Contents

POPULAR ENGLISH IDIOMS AND PHRASES 1
Dedication 2
Copyright Notice 3

English Idioms and Phrases -- A 5
English Idioms and Phrases -- B 9
English Idioms and Phrases -- C 17
English Idioms and Phrases -- D 24
English Idioms and Phrases -- E 28
English Idioms and Phrases -- F 32
English Idioms and Phrases -- G 37
English Idioms and Phrases -- H 40
English Idioms and Phrases -- I 47
English Idioms and Phrases -- J, K 48
English Idioms and Phrases -- L 50
English Idioms and Phrases -- M 55
English Idioms and Phrases -- N 59
English Idioms and Phrases -- O 62
English Idioms and Phrases -- P, Q 64
English Idioms and Phrases -- R 70
English Idioms and Phrases -- S 74
English Idioms and Phrases -- T 84
English Idioms and Phrases -- U, V 90
English Idioms and Phrases -- W-Z 92

About the Author 97
BIBLIOGRAPHY 98

English Idioms and Phrases -- A

ADD

001. -- State governments should **add more teeth** to anti-ragging laws. *['add more teeth' -- to make something more effective]*

002. -- Financial issues are further going to **add to their woes**.

ABACK

003. -- He appeared to be **taken aback** when it was revealed to him that an avid fan had his face tattooed on his arm. || We all were **taken aback** by bomb attacks. *['taken aback' -- very surprised]*

ACE

004. -- Our opponents **hold all the Aces** as they are strong where we are weak. *['hold all the aces' -- to have all the advantages]*

ACCOUNT

005. -- **From all accounts**, he was a loving family man. || **From all accounts**, he is a smart, fair-minded, detail-oriented middle-of-the-road jurist. *['from all accounts' -- according to what other people say]*

ACT

006. -- An accidental fire in your home is not considered an **act of God** because it could have been prevented. *['act of God' -- an event that is caused by natural forces]*

ADVANCE

007. -- The celebration started a day **in advance**. *['in advance' -- ahead of time]*

AFFAIR

008. -- Budget data revealed an alarming **state of affairs**. *['state of affairs' -- situation]*

009. -- My birthday is going to be **a quiet affair** with a nice dinner. || We want our wedding to be **a quiet affair**.

AGREE

010. -- Democracy requires that we **agree to differ**. *['agree to differ' -- (of people) to decide not to argue with each other over their different opinions about something.]*

AIR

011. -- Her clarification did not **clear the air**. *['clear the air' -- to improve a tense situation]*

012a. -- When the residents started receiving mysterious threats, there was an **air of mystery and fear**.

012b. -- The **air of celebration** was evident outside the president's office.

013a. -- It was fortunate that he arrived and erased the **negativity in the air**.

013b. -- There was an **evil smell in the air**.

014a. -- Body is nothing but a pile of ashes and it will one day **disappear into thin air**.

014b. -- Money was **vanishing into thin air**.

015. -- Many buses are plying in the city **throwing all norms to the air** and caring the least for people's lives.

ALL

016. -- I do not think we will be paying much more **if at all** we do.

017. -- If you stop her doing anything, she wants to do it **all the more**. *['all the more' -- extra]*

018. -- These problems are needed to be solved **once and for all**. *['once and for all' -- forever]*

019. -- **All of a sudden**, there was a fire. | **All of a sudden** a warm gust of wind came. *['all of a sudden' -- surprisingly]*

020. -- I learnt computer programming **all by myself**. || It is a lot of work, and I do it **all by myself**. || He had to run the family **all by himself**.

ALONE

021. -- Workers were clearly in no mood to listen **let alone** comply with the request. || They could not figure out how to punish corrupt officials, **let alone** fix them. *['let alone' -- used to emphasize that because the first thing is not true, possible, etc. the next thing cannot be true, possible, etc. either]*

APART

022. -- A saddle tank on the tractor-trailer **came apart** and caused a diesel spill. *['come apart' -- to shatter]*

023. -- In less than a fortnight of its formation, the Joint Committee for drafting the bill is **falling apart**. || Talks on a deal finally **fell apart**. *['fall apart' -- to collapse]*

024. -- Storm has **torn apart** the lives of thousands of people. *['tear apart' -- to destroy]*

025. -- We are **poles apart**. || Two exhibitions in prominent galleries immediately next to each other showed works that were **poles apart** in concept. *['pole apart' -- completely opposite]*

APPLE

026. -- We expected him to keep his business affairs **in apple-pie order**. || Everything inside the shop was spick and span and **in apple-pie order**, from the well-polished service counters to the glistening display cabinets. *['in apple pie order' -- well organized]*

ARM

027. -- Government maintained **arm's length distance** in all matters relating to film certification. *['arm's length distance' -- to avoid having a close relationship]*

028. -- Nation welcomed new football coach **with open arms**. || European counties had welcomed the refugees **with open arms**. *['with open arms' -- in an extremely happy manner]*

029. -- We need to bring about a system where access to justice doesn't **cost an arm and a leg**. *['cost an arm and a leg' -- to be too expensive]*

030. -- They are **up in arms** against each other for quite some time. *['up in arms' -- to be very angry and protesting strongly]*

AS

031. -- **As of now** I have not thought of it. || We have not come across any such complaint **as of now**.

032. -- Other details of the plan will be disclosed to you **as and when** required. *['as and when' -- something may happen in the future, but only when something else has happened]*

033. -- Administrative sources said that schools, clinics would continue on an **'as is where is' basis** in residential areas.

AWAY

034. -- Security checks at the airport cannot be done **away with**. | Should we do **away with** 5 days working week? | Do **away with** the country's reputation as being tourist-unfriendly. *['away with' -- to get rid of]*

English Idioms and Phrases -- B

BACK

035. -- Farmers are **back on the streets** demanding agriculture reforms.

036. -- He won two medals **back-to-back**. *['back-to-back' -- one after the other]*

037. -- The ring of a landline phone could clearly be heard **in the background**.

038. -- Our guide knew the monument **like the back of his hand**. *['like the back of somebody's hand' -- to be very familiar]*

039. -- My close relatives went on a foreign tour **behind my back**. *['behind somebody's back' -- without somebody's knowledge or permission.]*

040. -- Fare has been hiked **through the backdoor**. *['through the backdoor' -- using indirect or secret means]*

041. -- There is no **backdoor** and **open door talks** with anyone.

042. -- I do not **look back** in life.

043. -- They **turned back the pages to the early years** of the sixteenth century. || Just **turn back the pages of history** and you will find many examples where one vote has determined the winner of an election.

044. -- They resolved to **break the back** of the enemy. || We pray that God will **break the backs** of those who oppose humanity. || Army **broke the back** of terrorist groups. *['break the back' -- to conquer completely]*

045. -- Unfortunately, after the transfer of the DM, things **went into the backburner**. *['go into the backburner' -- to be postponed]*

046. -- The electorate was deeply divided into religious and caste lines, and issues of development **had taken a back seat**. *['had taken a back seat' -- played less important role than something else]*

BACKBONE

047. -- City buses and tempos **form the backbone** of public transport in many cities. || Infrastructure is the **backbone** of any nation's development and quality of life. || Energy availability and efficiency is the **backbone** of a

developing economy. *['form the backbone' -- to become the most important part]*

BAD

048. -- This player is the **best of a bad bunch**! *['best of a bad bunch' -- a little better than the rest of a group]*

049. -- Books of my colleague were in **bad shape**. *['bad shape' -- poor condition]*

BAG

050. -- She seemed to be shrinking and was reduced to **a bag of bones**. || Back in his childhood days, he was **a bag of bones**. *['a bag of bones' -- very thin person]*

BALL

051a. -- Legislators had tried to **lob the ball in** Prime Minister's court. *['lob the ball' -- to make somebody responsible for something]*

051b. -- Now **ball is in the** government's court. *[= It is the government's responsibility to take action next]*

BANG

052. -- I will be back **with a bang**. || Grand Slam champion is set to make a comeback in the forthcoming season **with a bang**. *['with a bang' -- successfully]*

BARK

053. -- He is **barking up the wrong tree** if he is going up to his enemies for help. || By suspecting his involvement in the conspiracy, the investigators were **barking up the wrong tree**. *['bark up the wrong tree' -- to have the wrong idea about how to get desired results.]*

BATTLE

054. -- She **fought a losing battle** with endometrial cancer. || As cities around the county are **fighting a losing battle** against floods, researchers are discovering ways to predict future natural disasters. *['fight a loose battle' -- to try to do something that you probably never succeed in]*

BEAR

055. -- The ruling party may have to **bear the brunt** of people's anger. || Automobile sector continued to **bear the brunt** of negative consumer sentiments. || The city **bore the brunt** of the natural disaster. *['bear the brunt' -- receive the unpleasant impact]*

BED

056. -- Our lives cannot be like a **bed of roses** with no obstacles and hindrances. *['like a bed of roses' -- extremely pleasant]*

BELT

057. -- Hunter had 48 leopard scalps **under his belt.** *['to have under your belt' -- to have achieved]*

BEND

058. -- Development Authority **bent rules** to allot prime plots.

059. -- When you **bend the truth**, it creates anxiety and can negatively affect your performance. || Some people **bend the truth** because they want to seem more desirable or cool. *['bend the truth' -- to say something that is only partially true.]*

BENEATH

060. -- He thinks the clerical **job is beneath him**. *[= not good enough for him]*

BEYOND

061a. -- She was intelligent **beyond belief**.

061b. -- Some things are **beyond punishment**.
061c. -- I am grateful to him **beyond words.**

BIRD
062a. -- Are you a *night owl* or **an early bird**? *['early bird' -- a person who wakes up very early]*
062b. -- Those registering for the conference by May 10 will receive **an early-bird** discounted rate of $100. *['early bird' -- a person who arrive or do something very early]*
063. -- A **bird's eye view** of the budget did not reveal any clear-sighted approach to transforming the economy. *['a bird's eye view' -- an overall or cursory look at something.]*

BLOOD
064. -- A good book is the **life-blood** of its author.
065. -- Travelling is **in my blood** from birth.
066. -- Business **ran in his blood**, and he could never keep himself away from work. *['be In somebody's blood' -- to be a natural part of somebody's character]*
067. -- Is it possible to love a robot more than **your own flesh and blood**? *['your own flesh and blood' -- your relatives]*
068. -- The **blood, sweat and tears** of artisans and laborers went into the making of White House. *['blood, sweat and tears' -- a lot of effort]*

BLUE
069. -- Security forces sometimes **beat** protestors **black and blue**. || The two boys pounced on the robber and **beat** him **black and blue**. || Police pulled them down and **thrashed** them **black and blue**. *['beat, thrash, etc. black and blue' -- to hit severely]*
070. -- **Out of the blue**, someone asked him what his views are on nuclear energy as an environmentalist. *['out of the blue' -- unexpected]*
071. -- She was crying miserably, her **body turning blue and cold.**

BOMB
072. -- He was a **ticking bomb** ready to go off.

BONE
073. -- The Kohinoor diamond has been a **bone of contention** between the Indian and the British governments for decades. || Water woes have become a major **bone of contention** between villagers and administration. *['bone of contention' -- a subject or issue over which there is continuing dispute]*

BOOK
074. -- A realtor should be **an open book** when it comes to showing you a house. || His music, and life, have always been **an open book**. || I have made myself **an open book** for everybody. *['an open book -- somebody/something that is easy to understand or about which everything is known.]*

BOON
075. -- Nuclear power is **a boon if used** for welfare and **a bane if used** for destruction.

BORN
076. -- He was **born an American** and **died an American**.
077. -- Common man is a **born loser** in some countries. *['born loser' -- always unsuccessful]*

BOTTOM
078. -- It is an ongoing investigation and they are doing the best they can to **get to the bottom of** it. || We need to **get to the bottom of** all the issues. *['to get to the bottom of something' -- to discover the main cause of something unpleasant]*

BOX

079. -- Some exams require the students to **think out of the box** and get out of their comfort zone. || It is not too late for the company to **think out of the box** to revive itself. || Politicians need to **think out of the box** to find remedies and answers for the problems faced by the people. || He has the intellectual capacity and engineering excellence to create and **think outside of the box**. *['think outside of the box' -- to think differently]*

BREAD

080. -- Nowadays our captain's **bread is buttered**. *['bread is buttered' -- to have in a position of advantage]*

081. -- **Millions of** people are unable to buy their **daily bread**. *['daily bread' -- the basic things for a living]*

BREATH

082. -- We waited for the announcement of the winner **with bated breath**. *['with bated breath' -- worriedly]*

083. -- He **held** his **breaths** waiting for her response. || The world **held** its **breath**. *['hold breath' -- to be very worried]*

084. -- She is a great artist but her husband's name is seldom taken **in the same breath**. *['in the same breath' -- used to show opposite meaning]*

085. -- He muttered **under his breath**, asking the protestors to shut up.

086. -- We need the **breath of life** that only good businesses can bring us. *['breath of life' -- the most important part of existence]*

BRICK

087. -- Do not go down on people **like a ton of bricks**. *['like a ton of bricks' -- very severely]*

088. -- We have taken an oath that we will **answer every brick with a rock**. *['answer every brick with a rock' – in an appropriate way]*

BRICKBAT

089. -- We should learn to accept the **brickbats with the bouquets**. *['brickbats with the bouquets' -- both pleasant and unpleasant things together]*

BRIDGE

090. -- The **bridge between** police **and** intelligence work has to be more effective.

091. -- There is a need to **bridge the gap** between established organizations and emerging businesses. *['bridge the gap' -- to reduce the differences]*

BRIGHT

092. -- Do you still manage to always **look on the bright side** of layoffs? || I am the kind of person who tries to **look on the bright side** of life. *['bright side' -- positive aspect]*

BROAD

093. -- That was the shocking moment a woman was mugged **in broad daylight** by a gang of children as passers-by walked by without intervening.

BUCKET

094. -- He **wept buckets** when his friend died.

BULLET

095. -- As the traffic gets worse in the national capital, now is the time for the current government to **bite the bullet**. || If I have to get something online I just get it in bulk and **bite the bullet** for shipping once. *['bite the bullet' -- to deal with an unpleasant and unavoidable situation]*

BURY

096. -- He was **buried under debt**.

097. -- Are the authorities deliberately trying to **bury this case**?

BUTTERFLY

098. -- It is common to **experience butterflies in the stomach** before any major life event. *['experience butterflies in the stomach' -- to have a nervous feeling in your stomach before doing something]*

English Idioms and Phrases -- C

CAP
099. -- Anytime you can beat a really good team it is definitely **a feather in your cap**. *['a feather in your cap' -- a respectful deed that you have done]*

CAPACITY
100. -- I will work **in the capacity** of a volunteer. || She was leaving for London in her **individual capacity**. || He will be present there **in his capacity as** president of the association. || He was transferred to the department of national integration **in the same capacity**. *['in the capacity' -- in the role]*

CARD
101. -- A flyover collapsed like a **house of cards**.

CARE
102. -- They have not **the least care** in the world. || If you have a busy life, the pet you get should be the breed that requires **the least care** and effort for maintenance.

CARROT
103. -- Addressing a large crowd, PM **dangled a number of carrots** for the poll-bound state in his speech. *['dangled a number of carrots' -- offered many things to somebody with a view to persuade them to do something]*

CART
104. -- Not to **put the cart before the horse**, he is just starting to fundraise, with $5,000 collected so far. || Winning the last four games is very possible but let's not **put the cart before the horse**. *['put the cart before the horse' -- to do something in the order which is incorrect]*

CASE
105. -- Various measures are in place **in case of an emergency**.

CAST
106a. -- Do not **cast a slur** upon your family. *['cast a slur' -- to insult]*
106b. -- Should we **cast aspersions on** Parliament? || We are in no position to **cast aspersions** on the judgment of the court. *['cast aspersions' -- to say critical remarks]*

CAT
107. -- It was kind of **a cat-and-mouse game** where I was constantly being attacked and defending my own position against my opponents. || Army men and terrorists often play **a cat and mouse game** with each other.
108. -- She had taken the lead in "**belling the cat**" *['belling the cat' -- try to do a seemingly impossible task.]*

CATCH
109. -- His action **caught** her **by surprise**.
110. -- A masked man **caught red-handed** on camera taking a motorbike from the college campus. *['catch somebody red-handed -- to discover someone in the act of doing something bad, wrong or illegal]*

CAUSE
111. -- Do not leave the **cause of freedom**.
112. -- Polluted water is the **root cause of the** spread of diseases.
113. -- Scandal **caused an earthquake** in the country's politics.

CENTER (CENTRE)
114a. -- The officer in question has always been **at the center of controversy**.

114b. -- She found herself **at the center of a national debate** about free speech and racial sensitivity.

CHANCE
115. -- He has said there is a **fifty-fifty chance** he will retire when his current five-year contract expires.

CHANGE
116a. -- The **momentum of change** is building.
116b. -- The **pace of change** in the world is increasing.
116c. -- There has been **a sea of change**.
116d. -- **Winds of change** are blowing through our economy. || The **winds of change** have begun to blow across the political landscape.

CHANNEL
117. -- Union members filed a grievance about the pay several years ago but they were denied because they did not **go through the proper channels**.

CHAPTER
118. -- PM visit **opened a new chapter** in ties between two countries. || They had **opened a new chapter** in history forming a genuine national government through consensus.

CHEW
119. -- We want to **chew them alive**. *['chew somebody alive' -- used to show you are very angry with somebody]*

CIRCLE
120. -- For him, life has **come full circle**. || With the DET party's withdrawal from the SPQ party today, history **turned full circle** 10 years after SPQ

pulled down the DET government. *['come/turn full circle' -- to return to the original situation]*

CLAIM
121. -- Police officers made **tall claims** of containing crimes. || Central minister was criticized for making **tall claims** and irresponsible statements.
122. -- There was no immediate **claim of responsibility** in a fierce attack.

CLOCK
123. -- World leaders were working **against the clock** to broker a deal that would stave off the most devastating effects of climate change. *['against the clock' -- before a particular time]*
124. -- We cannot **turn the clock back** now. *['turn the clock back' -- to return to the past situation]*
125. -- We worked **round the clock** for him. || Many cottages have **round the clock** hot water supply. *['round the clock' -- all day and all night without stopping]*

CLOSE
126. -- She was **holding the cards close to her chest**. *['hold cards close to your chest' -- to don't tell about your plans]*
127. -- Scientists **inched closer to scripting history**.

CLOUD
128. -- All faces were **clouded with worry**.
129. -- He is **on cloud nine** after his success. *['on cloud nine' -- extremely happy]*
130. -- The police theory of suicide has come **under a cloud**. || His leadership is already **under a cloud**. || The probe into the scam has brought **under cloud** two hospitals. || The pious relationship of a teacher and student should never **come under a dark cloud**. *['under a cloud' -- on suspicion]*

CLUTCH
131. -- You can't escape from **clutches of law**. || Can the rich **escape the clutches** of law even after committing a wrong!

COIN
132. -- They are just **two sides of the same coin.** || Theism and atheism are **two sides of the same coin**. || Winning and losing are **two sides of the same coin.** *['two sides of the same coin' -- two ways of looking at the same situation]*

COLD
133. -- **Cold water poured** over President's plans. *['pour cold water' -- to criticize; to bring to an end]*
134. -- He developed **cold feet on** seeing his rivals. *['to develop cold feet' -- to suddenly become nervous]*

COLLAPSE
135. -- The **world had collapsed** around her when his husband died.

COLOUR
136. -- **Religious color** was being given to the minor incident.
137. -- The **colors have gone from her life** after the death of her husband.

COME
138. -- Their differences **came to the fore.**
139. -- The latest news **came as a shock.** || Her move has **come as a shocker**.
140. -- We will **"come out clean"** in all the cases.
141. -- They think I will finally **'come to my senses.**
142. -- Every achievement **comes with a price**.

143. -- It seems comfort **comes first** for two-wheelers riders in the city and safety **distant second**.
144. -- No clue has **come to light** so far.
145. -- Victims struggled **to come to terms** with their painful memories.

COMMON
146. -- Many employees of the company shared a lot of **common ground**.

CONCEAL
147. -- He was **"concealing a lot"** in his statement.

CONDITION
148. -- "We may arrest the tainted lawyer", a senior official said **on condition of anonymity**.

CONTEXT
149. -- He has said so in **a general context**. || You are misjudging me unfairly when you take my remarks out of a **general context**.
150a. -- He responded that his **words** had been **taken out of context**.
150b. -- He was **quoted out of the context**.

CORE
151. -- Terrorist attacks shake society **to its core**. *['to its core' -- wholly]*

CORNER
152. -- Winter is just **around the corner**. || The next deadline is again **round the corner**. || His end was **round the corner**. || Elections are **round the corner**. || Winter vacations are **round the corner**. *['round (around) the corner' -- very near]*

COUNT

153. -- Entire town was affected with high voltage and people have been suffering losses **on this count**. || The work is in progress **on this count**.

CRACK
154. -- The government **cracked the whip** on mushrooming of ultra-sound clinics, closing 100 of them. || Police have **cracked the whip** on those who can create trouble during the polls. || Transport department is **cracking the whip** against people who are using red or blue beacons atop their vehicles without authorization. || Police **cracked the whip** on teachers' stir. *['crack the whip' -- to use your authority forcefully]*

CRY
155. -- She broke out into loud **cries of joy**.
156. -- There is no use **crying over it** now.
157. -- There was a **hue and cry** over the rising incidents of intolerance in the country. *['hue and cry' -- strong public protest or agitation]*
158. -- Twenty technicians in the company **cried foul** after being served with a termination notice. || Budget hotel operators **cried foul** over the council's additional fee. *['cry foul' -- to complain of unfair treatment]*

CURTAIN
159. -- **Curtains came down** on Thursday on the five-phase assembly election, with over half of the 20 million electorates turned out to vote in the final round. *['curtain came down' -- to mark the end of something]*

CUT
160. -- She **cut a sorry/striking figure** on the stage. *['cut a ... figure' -- to have a particular appearance]*
161. -- While he was speaking, his teacher **cut him short**. *['cut somebody short' -- to interrupt]*

English Idioms and Phrases -- D

DARKNESS
162. -- **There is darkness all around** these poor families. *[= the state of complete hopelessness]*

DAY
163. -- He has to work **night and day** to feed his family. *['night and day' -- continually]*

DEATH
164. -- Domestic violence is **a matter of life and death**. || Is football **a matter of life and death?** || The slightest error on the part of a driver can be **a matter of life and death** for travelers. *['a matter of life and death' -- extremely important or serious situation]*

165. -- It was a slow and painful **death of great expectations**.

DEAF
166. -- Health department was behaving **deaf and dumb**. *['deaf and dumb' -- neglectful]*

167. -- The demand to beautify the park has **fallen on deaf ears**. *['fall on deaf ear' -- to be ignored or unnoticed]*

168. -- **Turning a deaf ear** will not sort out the problem. *['turn a deaf ear' -- to refuse to listen to somebody/something]*

DEAL
169. -- Restrictions on travel could hurt the tourism industry and **deal a blow** to the economy. *['deal a blow' -- to be very harmful.]*

170. -- Controversy is **no big deal** for many celebrities. *['no big deal' -- no need to worry]*

171. -- Officials fret over a **raw deal** to State in disaster relief funds. *['raw deal' -- unfair treatment]*

DECENCY
172. -- Both the parties crossed all limits of **decency and decorum**.

DECISIVE
173. -- We are in a **decisive phase** in which the return to stability is imminent. || The negotiations have entered a **decisive phase** and meetings are on to resolve differences.

DEEP
174. -- When we took the reports of the water and air to health experts, all of them said we are **in deep water**." *['in deep water(s)' -- in trouble or difficult situation]*

DESPAIR
175. -- The truth is that the longer we take to address our problem, the more we drift towards **an abyss of despair**.

DESTINY
176. -- It was **in our destiny** to meet again. || We may well have no say **in our destiny** at all.

DISPOSAL
177. -- He has a lot of material wealth **at his disposal** *(= available for use as he prefers)*.

DO
178. -- Our team had to face a **do-or-die** situation as we confronted hosts in the final.
179. -- Such excuses **will not do** here.

DOCK

180. -- Commission has put civic agencies **in the dock**. *[= on trial]*

DOOR

181. -- Misfortune had **knocked on the doors of** the real estate business. || They had been **knocking on the doors of** justice for the last 18 years. || With summers **knocking on the doors**, the use of air conditioners and coolers will increase. || With the rainy season **knocking at the doors** of the Uttarakhand state, the Jim Corbett tiger reserve, known for its elephant population, will be closed for tourists tomorrow onward.

182. -- The court ruled that his trial will be conducted **behind closed doors**. || Talks have resumed **behind closed doors** as lawmakers try to come to an agreement on a state budget. *['behind closed doors' -- away from the public eye]*

183. -- We have **shown the door** to over 100 members for anti-club activities. *['to show the door' – to expel]*

184. -- He took his team to the **doorstep of victory** but failed to **unlock the door.**

DOWN

185. -- He was a **down-to-earth** leader. *['down to earth' -- practical and realistic]*

186. -- People go through **ups and downs**. || Overall, it was an **up and down** week. || Every company has its **ups and downs**. || Life is full **of ups and downs**. *['ups and downs' -- inconsistency]*

187. -- His world had come **crashing down**.

188. -- The issue of change minister **refused to die down**. *['refuse to die down' -- to not decrease or become less strong]*

189. -- That dark night still **sends** a humiliating **chill down** our **spine**. || The roar of the tiger would **send chills running down the spine** of visitors. || SMS **sent shivers down the spine** of them. *['send chill/shivers down the spine' -- to frighten in an exciting way]*

DRAG
190. -- The government was **dragging its feet** on allowing foreign investigators to probe the source of the attack. *['drag your feet' -- to be intentionally slow in doing something]*

DREAM
191. -- Desire without work is **daydreaming**. *['daydreaming' -- carelessness]*
192. -- He **weaves dreams** for others.
193. -- I have a **dream of my own**.
194. -- He said it was "**a dream come true**" arriving in London as a tourist.
195. -- Her decision to quit the job has made an impact far **beyond his wildest dream/imagination.**
196. -- The debt burden **crushed his dream** of peaceful life. || The wheels of a speeding bus **crushed the dreams** of an 18-year old student.
197. -- He was able to **carve out the life of his dreams**.

DRAIN
198. – All his efforts have just **gone down the drain**. *['to go down the drain' -- to be wasted completely]*

DROP
199. -- President **dropped a bombshell** when he said he was quitting his post. || Our captain has **dropped a bombshell** by saying our team did not deserve to be champions. *['drop a bombshell' -- to give unexpected and very unpleasant information]*

DUST
200a. -- Hundreds of computers were **gathering dust** in government offices. *['gathering dust' -- not being used]*
200b. -- The inquiry report is said to be **getting dust** with the government.

English Idioms and Phrases -- E

EAR

201. -- It is unwise to **shut your ears to** opinions that differ from yours. [*'shut your ears to something' -- to not listen to something*]

202. -- We open our ears only to make sure that words we do not agree with **go in one ear and out the other**. || When you simply memorize something, it tends to **go in one ear and out the other**. || You can talk bad about me and I promise, it can just **go in one ear and out the other**. [*'go in one ear and out the other' -- to be forgotten soon*]

EARTH

203. -- We will **move heaven and earth** to make sure she gets justice. [*'move heaven and earth' -- to make maximum efforts to achieve something*]

EAT

204. -- Religious **terrorism is eating us** from the inside.

EDGE

205. -- There are moments in history when the future of a nation balances **on a knife-edge**. || He is like **living on a knife-edge**. || The survey found the result of the crucial ballot on June 23 is **on a knife-edge** - with those who had decided which way to vote split 50-50. [*'on a knife edge' -- finely balanced between success and failure*]

206. -- Every good and excellent thing in the world stands moment by moment **on the razor's edge** of danger. || His future is **poised on the razor's edge**. || Cars and drivers are always **on the razor's edge** and are expected to give 100% at all times. [*'on the razor's edge' -- to be in a critical and difficult situation.*]

EFFECT

207. -- He has been banned from playing in international cricket **with immediate effect** by the International Cricket Council.

ELBOW
208. -- There is a lot of **jostling and elbowing**. *['jostling and elbowing' -- forceful competition]*

END
209. -- The common people are unable to **make both ends meet** due to skyrocketing prices of essential commodities. || In his meager salary, he finds it extremely hard to **make both ends meet**. || Many boxers have to do things other than professional boxing to **make both ends meet**. || In order to **make both ends meet,** they were forced to borrow money and very often, the employers would lend money to them. *['make both ends meet' -- to somehow manage to earn for your daily needs]*

210. -- Football coach found himself **on the receiving end** of some "tricky" questions from the audience. *['be on the receiving end' -- to be the person that has to deal with an unpleasant action]*

ENTER
211. -- I did not **enter into an argument** with them.
212. -- Compliment never **entered her mind.**

EQUAL
213. -- Four-five people have been saved **by an equal number of** villagers. || Ten terrorists and an **equal number of** security personnel were killed in the encounter.

214. -- His statement drew both admiration and criticism **in equal measures.**

EXHIBITION

215. -- It is not the case that he set out to **make an exhibition of himself**. *['make an exhibition of yourself' -- to behave very badly in public]*

EYE

216. -- Teachers should have **eyes at the back of their heads**. *['have eyes in the back of your head' -- to be able to notice something completely]*

217. -- He is an **apple of** my **eye**. *['apple of somebody's eye' -- that is loved very much]*

218. -- Banquet halls knowingly **turned a blind eye** to the safety precautions. || Cops present around the monument **turned a blind eye** to the activities of the tourist guides. || Police have **turned a blind eye** to my complaints. || While in politics, at times, it may be necessary **to turn a blind eye** towards a few things. || The authorities **turned a blind eye** even after he sent them a legal notice. *['turn a blind eye' -- to ignore something bad]*

219. -- He was looking at us with **wonder-struck eyes**.

220. -- Her **eyes were sparkling** with excitement.

221. -- The villagers have been asked to **keep an eye** on their children when they are visiting fields or playing near the river. *['keep an eye' -- to take care of somebody]*

222. -- How can things change **in the blink of an eye**? || **In the blink of an eye**, he went from planning a surprise birthday party to grasping the reality of putting together a funeral. || **In the blink of an eye**, the year is almost over. || So many years seemed to have flown by **in the blink of an eye**. *['In the blink of an eye' -- quickly]*

223. -- It was a prediction that **hit the bulls' eye**. *[= to be very accurate]*

224. -- She walked into the kitchen, **rubbing her sleep out of her eyes**.

225. -- Media forms the **eyes and ears** as far as citizens are concerned.

226. -- **Sparks danced** before his **eyes** when he saw a snake in his bedroom. *[= to be extremely scared and worried]*

227. -- Officials concerned with organizing tournaments are **keeping a hawk eye** over arrangements. || Administration and police are **keeping a**

hawk eye over proceedings to ensure no nuisance during the festival. || Election commission is **keeping a hawk-eye** on all sensitive centers.
['keep a hawk eye' -- to be able to notice everything]

228. -- The **pain and agony are visible in the eyes and voices** of these youths.

229. -- Voters said they **did not see eye-to-eye** with the president about the meat ban. || The treasury and opposition benches **did not see eye-to-eye** with each other throughout the session.

English Idioms and Phrases -- F

FACE

230. -- He shut the door **on my face**.

231. -- I know him **by face and not by name**.

232. -- Senior officers of the electricity department may have to **face the music** for recurrent electrical faults. *['face the music' -- to deal with criticism for wrongdoing]*

233. -- In some parts of the world, people do not want **to lose face** or show weakness. || They **lost face** because of you. *['to lose face' -- to be humiliated]*

234. -- On hearing his criticism, his **white face turned a shocking pink**.

235. -- Military personnel should display courage **in the face of** extreme odds. *['in the face of' -- despite]*

FAIR

236. -- The auction was held **fair and square.** || All they want is to share the airspace **fair and square** with other flying aircraft. || He truly wanted people to be aware that he won his matches **fair and square**. *['fair and square' -- according to the rules]*

237. -- It appeared that the government was intending to win the referendum **by fair means or foul**. *['by fair means and foul' -- using both right or wrong ways]*

FALL

238. -- **Axe might fall on** some officers for their negligence in preparing the report. *[= to be dismissed]*

239. -- He soon **fell under suspicion**.

240. -- High-debt companies may **fall like flies**.

241. -- Resolution **fell to the ground** for want of support.

242. -- Scheme **fell flat**. *['fall flat' -- to not have intended effect]*

243. -- Task of raising her four children **fell squarely** on her shoulders. *['fall squarely' -- directly]*

244. -- Anyone can **fall prey** to conmen in an unknown city. *['fall prey' -- to be affected by something bad]*

FAME

245. -- He was willing to sacrifice his happiness **on the altar of fame.** *['on the altar of something' -- because of something]*

246. -- Some celebrities have **risen to fame** for being associated with famous personalities.

247. -- Everyone loves an overnight success story, but **fame and fortune** far more often follow years of hard work. || Artists from all over the world come here to find **fame and fortune**.

FAN

248. -- We can't support those who are **fanning up** violence.

249. -- It is despicable and dangerous for presidential candidates to **fan the flames of hate**.

FAR

250. -- Company's proposals did not **go far enough.**

251. -- **Food was far** from his mind.

252. -- They are **far far ahead**. *[= have made a lot of progress]*

253. -- We have left them **far behind** in development.

254a. -- The situation was **far from smooth**. *[far from something -- almost opposite]*

254b. -- His work was **far from appreciated.**

254c. -- The reports in media in this regard are **far from the truth**.

255. -- The problem for shareholders was that they were by **far and away** the last parties to be paid anything in bankruptcy. || History shows that those societies with a vibrant culture are also, **far and away**, the most scientifically inventive. *['far and away' -- by a very great amount]*

256. -- Since the news of the king's death, fans **far and wide** have been crying purple tears. || Boston has seen its fair share of tourists, many of whom have traveled from **far and wide**. || Everything a President does reverberate **far and wide.** *['far and wide' -- over a large area]*

257. -- In my neighborhood locals look out for one another and crimes are **few and far between**. *[few and far between' -- not happening often]*

FATE
258. -- **Fate has dealt** him **a cruel blow.**

FINE
259. -- All the tourists are **"fine and safe."**

FIRE
260. -- This is not the first time they have **come under fire** for violating the traffic laws. || PM **came under fire** for her lackluster response to the earthquake disaster. *['come under fire' -- to be criticized]*

FISH
261. -- It is said that **small fish are easier to catch**. *[= to put the blame for wrongdoing on somebody who is at the lower level of* the *hierarchy]*

262. -- These players have **other fish to fry** for the time being. || I have never really been affected by criticism, as I **have other fish to fry**. *['have other fish to fry' -- to have more important things to do]*

FIT
263. -- His progress as a musician came **by fits and starts**. *['by fits and starts' -- not continuously]*

FLAG
264. -- They raised the **flag of revolt** against their organization.

FLY

265. -- He passed his evaluation period **with flying colors**. || At the examination he **came off with flying colors**. *['with flying colors' -- extremely well]*

266. -- Frequent incidents of robberies have seen **tempers flying** in the surrounding areas.

FOOT

267. -- All of them were **in bare feet**. *['in bare feet' -- not wearing shoes or socks]*

268. -- He is **back on his feet** again after suffering from a heat attack a few months ago. *['back on your feet' -- in a normal situation after facing a time of trouble]*

FRACTION

269. -- It all happened in **a fraction of a second**. || There will be no power cut here in the future even for a **fraction of a second**.

FREE

270. -- He had quit a job **out of her own free will**. || I have come here **of my own free will**. || She had married of her **own free will**.

FREEZE

271a. -- Then what he saw **froze him with fear**.

271b. -- Spectators **froze in horror** when they heard three blasts in succession.

FRONT

272. -- We need to fight terrorism **on every front**. || They accused that the government had failed **on every front** including law and order. || We are **strong on every front**.

FRUIT

273. -- Some of his efforts may have **borne fruit**. *['bear fruit' -- to be successful]*

FIRE

274. -- The **fire of jealousy** had been **frying** her.

275. -- News of their arrest **spread like wildfire** in the district.

FUEL

276. -- Spiraling prices have **added fuel to the fire**. *['add fuel to the fire' -- to worsen a situation]*

FULL

277. -- She slapped him **in full public view**. || Prime Minister rebuked the security officer **in full public view**.

278. -- The gun battle was **in full force**. || Winter weather is **in full force**.

FUN

279. -- He has brought shame on himself and for a while, he will become a **figure of fun** among the international community too. || She has become a **figure of fun** because she makes funny faces. *['become a figure of fun' -- to do something ridiculous]*

English Idioms and Phrases -- G

GAME
280. -- A road accident triggered a **blame game** among political rivals.

GENERAL
281. -- They should redraft gun laws in the country **in general** and in the capital **in particular.**

GEAR
282. -- Both sides struggled to **get into gear** in the early stages of the match. *['get into gear' -- to become very active or productive]*
283. -- Life has been **thrown** completely **out of gear** this season due to the erratic power and water supply. || Soaring mercury across the state has **thrown life out of gear.** *['be thrown out of gear' -- to be out of control]*
284. -- Opposition parties decided to put their campaign for assembly polls **in top gear** by fielding several of its frontline leaders. *['in top gear' -- in the most efficient way]*

GIVE
285. -- I know how to **give tit for tat.** *['give tit for tat' -- to exact revenge]*
286. -- Monsoon (a period of heavy rain in South Asia) may come in May – **give or take four days in error.**
287. -- He **gave** me **a flat refusal** when I sought his help.
288. -- Investors **gave thumbs-up** to the decision of the bank association.
289. -- Actress **gave** photographers **the slip** as she came with her head covered.

GLASS

290. -- Ex-director of the company was pressed about **which shards of glass had cut him** deepest during his 30 years in the company.

GLOOM
291. -- **Pall of gloom** descended on the areas when the bodies of the youths were brought to their homes.

GOOD
292. -- Cartoon published by the newspaper was not **in good taste**. *['in good taste' -- acceptable]*
293. -- He has done **one good** for the country.
294. -- She thought education would **do** his son **a lot of good.**
295. -- To live alone can **cause more harm than good.**
296. -- This decision is **for our good**.
297. -- You have to **take the bad with the good** and handle both graciously.

GRASP
298. -- He failed to **grasp the gravity** of the situation.

GREASE
299. -- Many officers are alleged to have **greased the palms** of politicians. *['grease the palm' -- to bribe]*

GREAT
300. -- We participate in sports gatherings **great and small**. || The energy transformation should touch all parts of society and economies, both **great and small.**

GREEN

301. -- The princesses **became green with jealousy.**

GRIP
302. -- **Football fever gripped** the world during the world cup.

GUN
303. -- Businessmen **trained their guns** on the minister and his party. || Opposition parties on Sunday **trained their guns** on the Government in the State over the question paper leak incident.

English Idioms and Phrases -- H

HABIT
304. -- A lot of people have been voting for this party **out of habit** and not really paying attention to the obvious changes. || Every time you are doing something **out of habit**, you do not think too much about it.

HAIR
305. -- I do not believe in **hair-splitting**. *['hair-splitting' -- too much attention in small details]*

306. -- We felt like **tearing out our hair.** || Investigators are still **tearing out their hair** about how much more money that they are not even knowing about. *['tear out your hair' -- to be extremely worried or confused]*

HALE
307. -- Former military chief has said that he is **hale and hearty.** *['hale and hearty' -- strong and healthy]*

HAND
308. -- Autonomy and accountability **go hand in hand.** || Praise and criticism **go hand in hand** for them. || Terror and midnight **go hand in hand**. *['hand in hand' -- together; closely related]*

309. -- DIMTS **washed** its **hands of** the shooting incident. || He has managed to **wash his hands of** the treachery. || She **washed her hands** of the whole matter. *['wash your hands of somebody/something' -- to decide not to involve in the matter]*

310. -- He had **joined hands with** her opponents. || He requested his friends to **join hands with** him and become a part of his campaign. *['join hands with somebody' -- to work together]*

311. -- Matters **went out of hand.** || Sometimes things **go out of hand.** || How things suddenly **went out of hand** is what I cannot understand. *['go out of hand' -- to be out of control]*

312. -- The enemies of humanity need to be **dealt with iron hands** and firm resolve. *['dealt with iron hands' -- to control rigorously]*

313. -- It is a terrible thing to **have your hands tied** when dealing with certain aspects of your life. *['have your hands tied' -- to be unable to do something because of rules, restrictions, etc.]*

314. -- Their **case changed hands** under 12 judges.

315. -- We do not want the country to **get into the hands of** a single-family.

316. -- Three victims of the robbery incident claimed that the police were **hand-in-glove** with the accused. || People alleged that transport department officials were **hand-in-glove** with the sand contractors. *['hand in glove (with sb)' -- working together in a dishonest or an illegal act]*

317. -- You do **have your hands full** and it can be quite stressful at times. *['have your hands full' -- to be too busy]*

HARD

318. -- He **fought hard** till the end. || They have **fought hard** over the past seven years to make sure everybody gets a good education. *['fight hard' -- to try to achieve something while facing a lot of difficulties]*

319. -- When you **give a hard time** to a particular faction they hate you, but then when you **give a hard time** to the other faction, they love you. *['give a hard time to somebody' -- to intentionally make a situation difficult and unpleasant for somebody]*

HARVEST

320. -- Organizations that promote employee engagement also **reap the harvest** of employee satisfaction. || We may soon be ready to **reap the harvest** of our investment. *['reap the harvest' -- to benefit or suffer as a direct result of your actions.]*

HATRED

321a. -- Convert **winds of hatred** into those of love and compassion.

321b. -- **Walls of hatred** are being erected in the name of religion.

HAVE

322. -- I still **have it in me** to give a good speech. *['have it in you' -- to be capable of doing something]*

HEAD

323a. -- He is steeped in corruption **from head to toe**. || Local authorities were draped in scams **from head to foot**. *['from head to toe (foot)' -- entirely]*

323b. -- She was covered **from head to toe**. *['from head to toe' -- covering your whole body]*

324. -- His act had made him '**hang his head in shame**.

325. -- It is not **written on one's head** that he or she is an extremist.

326. -- I **cannot make head or tail** of what he is saying. || He **couldn't make head or tail** of what she wanted to convey. *['can't make head or tail of something' -- to be completely unable to understand something]*

327. -- Every time you **lose your head** with an employee, the office will take notice. || If you are easily angered, or can **lose your head** at a moment's notice, you should not buy a gun. *['to lose your head' -- to be unable to behave sensibly]*

328. -- Caste violence **reared its head** at the small village.

329. -- I knew I needed to **keep a cool head**, try to get myself out of trouble and stick to the game plan. *['keep a cool head' -- to stay calm in a difficult situation]*

330. -- His **head turned** by money. *[= to become arrogant]*

HEALTH

331. -- He is **in the pink of health**. *[= good health]*

332. -- He was a **pillar of health and happiness**. *['pillar of something' -- somebody who has a lot of particular quality]*

333. -- She left the institute **on account of ill health.**

HEAP
334. -- Citizens of the country **heaped praise** on the scientists.

HEART
335. -- Bombing **rocked the heart** of the regime.

336a. -- Some of these people will be **etched on my heart** forever. || 14 April 1997, a date **etched on my memory**. || Her name will be **etched on my mind**. *['etch on your heart / memory / mind' -- to remember something that has highly impressed you]*

337. -- His photograph and names are **printed in our hearts**.

338. -- She is the **heartthrob of millions**.

339. -- When I came across news of his death, **my heart skipped a beat**.

340. -- These five days in this village really **touched my heart** and this experience has been very special to me, to say the least. *['to touch sb's heart' – to affect or concern sb a lot]*

341. -- His answers were **straight from the heart**.

342. -- Kitchen is the **heart of the home**.

343. -- He was a hard worker, he was generous, and he had **a heart of gold**. || He was always laughing and smiling, with a **heart of gold** and everyone who met him loved him straight away. *['a heart of gold' -- very kind and good nature]*

344. -- He has put his whole **heart and soul** into winning the competition. || He is one of the players that is like the **heart and soul** of this team. || The governor had **put** his "**heart and soul**" in making sure the state "bounce back stronger than before".

345. -- She loves him **from the bottom of her heart** and she is never afraid to show it. || If you are surrounded only by the items which you really love, you will feel the joy and happiness coming up **from the bottom of your heart**. || His behavior cemented the belief that he did not **speak from the bottom of his heart**. *['from the bottom of the heart' -- with sincere and deep feeling]*

346. -- Even the **stoniest of hearts melts** before flower. || You would need a **heart of stone** not to be moved by the plight of migrants as they tell of homelessness, overcrowding, sub-standard conditions, *['heart of stone' -- cold and unfeeling nature]*

347. -- His **heart is in pieces** after the death of his little daughter. *[= he is feeling devastated.]*

HEAT

348. -- They got into an argument that turned physical and injured each other in the **heat of passion**,

HEEL

349. -- He was **head-over-heels** in hate with his enemy. *['head-over-heels -- passionately]*

350. -- Bombers are now **cooling their heels** in jail.

HERE

351. -- He set out in search of peace, looking **here, there and everywhere** in all corners of the globe.

HIGH/HIGHT

352. -- Eating out habit is **on high**.
353. -- She was on a **new political high**.
354. -- Security is **at an all-time high.**
355. -- Shakespeare took English literature to **untouched heights**.

HIT

356. -- Investigators have **hit a wall** after a witness turned hostile. || The reform push has **hit a wall** of protest. *['hit a wall' -- to reach a point when you cannot continue something]*

357. -- People **hit the streets** against rising vegetable prices. *['hit the streets' -- to oppose something intensely]*

358. -- They got married 10 years ago, but their relationship **hit rough patches** for the past couple of months. *['hit rough patches' -- to worsen]*

HOLD
359. -- He has **held up a mirror** to state authorities. *['hold up a mirror' -- to show reality]*

360. -- Competition was fierce but the local team **held their heads high** and only lost one game and finished fourth overall. *['hold your heads high -- to be proud, not ashamed.]*

361. -- Grassroot leaders **hold sway** with a lot of voters. *['hold sway -- to have influence or power over sb.]*

362. -- His arguments do **not hold water**. || Assumptions and conjecture alone do **not hold water** and thus cannot lead to convictions. *['not hold water' -- not believable]*

HOLE
363. -- His death has left a **crater-sized hole in the heart** of his fans.

364. -- Investigating agency found **holes in the** state police **theory**. || **Hole in his argument** was deeper than imagined. || You do not have to be a professor of logic to see the **holes in his arguments**. *['to find, see or pick holes in something' -- to find weak points]*

HOLLOW
365. -- A lot of **hollow promises** have been made.

HOOK
366. -- They will not be **let off the hook** so easily. *['let off the hook' -- to be freed from blame or obligation]*

367. -- The odds are that **by hook or by crook** a deal will be struck. || Be wary of those who wish to take your money **by hook or by crook**. *['by hook or by crook' -- using honest or dishonest way]*

HOPE

368. -- Throughout the season we had **glimmers of hope** every now and again.

369. -- We should **ignite hope** among the earthquake-affected people.

370. -- State aid gave troubled shipyards a **ray of hope**.

HOT

371. -- My post is **neither hot nor cool**.

372. -- Her albums **sell like hot cakes**. *['sell like hot cakes' -- to sell in great numbers]*

HOUR

373. -- Police officials said they were informed about PM's visit **at the eleventh hour** and did not have enough time to make adequate preparations. || Officials were so unsure of the celebrations that even the invitation cards were printed **at the eleventh hour**. *['at the eleventh hour' -- at the last moment]*

HURT

374. -- He was a very friendly person and would never **hurt a fly**.

English Idioms and Phrases -- I

ICE

375. -- It did not take long for them to **break the ice** with their good-natured banter. || We were trying to **break the ice** and get him to feel comfortable with us. *['break the ice' -- to say or do something that makes people feel more relaxed.]*

IF

376. -- There are **ifs and buts** in the path to a cleaner city, all of which need to be addressed systematically. || I am not one of the cynics who always put **ifs and buts**. || Despite all the **ifs and buts** about it, the flu shot does reduce your chance of getting the flu. *['ifs and buts' -- confusion]*

INCH

377. -- **Every inch** of this house scares me. || She looked **every inch** the party princess as she donned a blue and red dress. || She looked **every inch** what she was, a senior person's PA.

378. -- He was **not** ready to **budge an inch** from its claim. || He said that they would **not budge an inch** from their indefinite agitation till their demands were met. || We shall **not budge an inch** in fulfilling our constitutional duty until the last moment. *['not budge an inch' -- to not change your position on something at any cost.]*

INSIDE

379. -- He is **cool on the outside but burning** for his country on the **inside**.

380. -- He knows every policy **inside and out**.

English Idioms and Phrases -- J, K

JAW
381. -- India snatched victory from **jaws of defeat**.
382. -- They pushed him into **jaws of certain death**. *['jaws of death' -- extremely unpleasant or horrific situation that is very difficult to avoid]*

JOKE
383. -- Nobody should **make a joke of** patriotism. *['make a joke of' -- to laugh at serious things]*

JUMP
384. -- Management **jumped into** damage control.
385. -- They should not **jump to any conclusion** before hearing out stakeholders.

KEEP
386. -- He was **kept in the dark** and got all the details pertaining to the case from the media. *['In the dark' -- knowing nothing about something]*

KEY
387. -- As with most things, planning ahead is the **key to success**.

KICK
388. -- Youth often **kick against the rules**.
389. -- They ran drug addiction programs that helped thousands of addicts **kick the habit**. *['kick the habit' -- to stop doing something harmful that you have done for a long time]*
390. -- It was like a **kick in the face** that made me realize I had to take a different approach while not compromising my ideals. *['kick in the face' -- a hurtful criticism]*

KID

391. -- You cannot **kid me**. || A working mother cannot **kid herself** that she can be in two places at once. *['to kid somebody' -- to deceive]*

KINDERED

392. -- She was looking for a **kindred spirit** among the masses. *['kindred spirit' -- a person with similar attitudes, interests, ideas, etc.]*

KNOT

393. -- As many as 210 couples of different castes **tied the knot** at a mass wedding ceremony. *['tie the knot' -- to get married]*

KNOW

394. -- Officials were promoting the plan for **reasons best known to them**.

395. -- It will help you learn to **know where you stand** on subjects and issues. *['know where you stand' -- to be aware of your situation]*

English Idioms and Phrases -- L

LAMB
396. -- Junior officers were being **made "sacrificial lamb"** in the large-scale chit-fund scam. *[= being blamed unfairly for something they did not do]*

LANGUAGE
397. -- The **language of music** should prevail over the **language of anger and hate**.

LARGE
398. -- Barring a few untoward incidents, polling was **by and large** peaceful. *['by and large' -- on the whole; in general; everything considered]*

LAUGH
399a. -- The whole world was **laughing at him**.
399b. -- He has turned our club into a **laughing stock**.
400. -- Threats made on social media are **no laughing matter**. || Politics is **no laughing matter**. *['no laughing matter' -- not a trivial issue]*

LIE/LAY
401. -- He **laid bare** his ambition for a national role. || The enemy's plan was **laid bare**. *['lay bare' -- to become known]*
402. -- They **laid the blame for** the war in Iraq **on** American **doors**.

LIFE
403. -- Roads are the **lifeline** of the hills.

LEAP
404. -- Farmers hope for **a big leap forward in** agriculture. *['a big leap forward' -- a great success]*

405. -- He is progressing **by leaps and bounds**. || Artificial intelligence has advanced by **leaps and bounds** in recent years. || We want them to make the progress by **leaps and bounds**. || Smartphone penetration is increasing by **leaps and bounds**, globally. || The freelance workforce is growing by **leaps and bounds**. *['by leaps and bounds' -- very fast]*

LEAVE

406. -- Defects in the new vehicle had already **left a bad taste in his mouth**. *['leave a bad taste in the mouth' -- to make you feel disgusted]*

407. -- He **left a stamp** of his own. || His presence and significance did not go unnoticed; He **left a stamp** and legacy, which is all he wanted to do.

408. -- Hoax bomb call **left** the police **in a sweat**.

LENGTH

409. -- Government would go through the recommendation **at length** before taking a final decision. || A team of NGOs spoke **at length** with one of the inmates of the orphanage. || We have interrogated him **at length** in our case. *['at length = in detail]*

410. -- They had traveled over 2 million miles "**through the length and breadth of the country**" campaigning against the corruption.

411. -- We will **go to any lengths** to ensure that the guilty are punished. *['go to any length' -- to put a lot of effort]*

LETTER

412. -- Try to implement your decision **in letter and spirit**. || They should ensure that the Land Ceiling Act is implemented **in letter and spirit**. || We must learn to respect the rights and sensitivities of minorities, both **in letter and spirit**.

LID

413. -- He **blew the lid off** the false encounter killing. *['blow the lid off' -- to tell the secret]*

LIEU
414. -- He pledged his jewelry **in lieu of** the loan. *['in lieu of' -- instead of]*

LIFE
415. -- We have the potential to **shine in every sphere of life.**
416. -- It is now a **set lifestyle** for them.
417. -- The horror of last week will haunt all of them for **the rest of their life**.
418. -- He thinks his misfortune is due to **sins committed in a past life**.
419. -- He has **escaped a bid on his life.**

LIGHT
420. -- She **threw** some **light** on the women literacy figures. || He **threw light** on the **pros and cons** of the scheme. || As he was the last person she interacted with before leaving the country, only he can **throw light on the** sequence of events. || President **threw light** on the constant demand and challenges of the judiciary.
421. -- She had her own major secrets, and it took more than twenty years for them to **see the light of day**. || People are often made to run from *pillar to post*, but they do not complain against any official for fear that their files will never **see the light of day**.
422. -- Road accidents often **put the spotlight** on the shoddy quality of road construction. *['put the spotlight' – to highlight]*
423a. -- Violent acts **take the light of** many people's lives and a family.
423b. -- It's my loved ones who **bring light into my life**.
424. -- He is trying hard to **light up the lives** of others.
425a. -- Governor of the state has **given the green light** to MCD's project. || The government **gave the green light** to a multi-million-dollar package of road repairs. *['give the green light' -- to give permission]*
425b. -- They were seeking to **get the green light** from authorities for the deal. *['get the green light' -- to get permission]*

LINE

426. -- Activists asked the officials to create a board **along the lines of** CBSE.

427. -- They wanted special classes, **in line with** those that had been devised in Washington.

428. -- He met with the president **on the sidelines of** the assembly meeting. *['on the sidelines of' -- without involving in the thing mentioned]*

429. -- This meeting should be looked at **on those lines** only.

430. -- It is important we do not **overstep the line**. || He has made it very clear throughout his whole presidency that he doesn't want anyone to **overstep the line**. *['overstep the line' -- to behave in an unacceptable way]*

431. -- We do not want **to toe the previous government's line** in this regard. *[= to follow]*

432. -- His warning didn't mention anyone by name, but it wasn't hard to **read between the lines**.

433. -- It is not always easy to know where to **draw the line** between something being 'normal' and 'harassment'. || It can sometimes be difficult to **draw the line** between legislative and judicial power. *['draw the line' -- to set a limit]*.

LIP

434. -- Many questions are **on the lips** of a lot of people.

LOCK

435. -- Government and opposition are still **locking horns over** the land issue. *['lock horns' -- to get involved in an argument or a disagreement with somebody]*

436. -- He will be kept **under lock and key** for the rest of his natural life. *['under lock and key' -- in jail]*

437. -- They are **locked in a confrontation** over land.

LONG

438. -- His statement is **long on promise but short on substance.**

439. -- You cannot escape the **long arm of the law.**

440. -- You have **given a long rope** to this boy. *['give a long rope' -- to give excessive freedom]*

441. -- It took him a long time to realize that cheap is usually more expensive **in the long run**.

442. -- Our association **goes back a long way** to almost three decades.

LOOSE

443. -- Neighbors **let loose their anger** at the culprit's house.

LOSE

444. -- Many companies are **losing their shine** in the global market.

445. -- In a war, **you win some, you lose some.**

446. -- His mother **lost track** of him at a shopping center.

447. -- She **lost** her **cool** and slapped her sister. || Passengers **lost their cool** while waiting in the serpentine queue to buy tickets. *['lose cool' -- to become angry or excited]*

LOSS

448. -- They are **at a loss of words** when the question of their point of origin arises. *['at a loss of words' -- not knowing what to say or do]*

English Idioms and Phrases -- M

MAKE

449. -- He is **making merry** these days. || Under the abandoned bunker, cattle were **making merry** by grazing on the small patch of grassy land.

450. -- He lost without **making it to the top**. | She lost after **making it to the top**.

451. -- They **made light of** my warning. || He tried to **make light of** the matter/situation. || Nobody should **make light of** such incidents. *['make light of something' -- to regard something as not much serious]*

452. -- His boss had "**made a fool**" of him.

453. -- People **made such a big issue** of a small incident.

454. -- She finally **made peace** with her husband. *['make peace' -- to end an argument by accepting your mistake]*

455. -- You are trying to **make a story out of something that is not a story**.

MAN

456. -- He is only **a 'yes man'**.

457. -- She is a **woman of limited means** and **many responsibilities**.

458. -- He proved to be successful in particular as a **man of action**.

MARK

459. -- Today is a holiday **as a mark of respect** for the departed soul. || The school has been closed, for the next two days **as a mark of respect** for those killed.

MATCH

460. -- She is **no match** for her friend at music. *['no match' -- not equal at all]*

MATTER

461a. -- Dying for their beliefs is a **matter of honor** for them.

461b. -- He resigned over a **matter of principle**.

462a. -- It was all over in a **matter of minutes**.

462b. -- So, it is only a **matter of time** before these birds vanish forever.

463. -- We were determined to **get to the root of the matter**.

464. -- Our failure was a **"matter of shame and regret"**.

MEAN

465. -- A young couple was accused to have tortured the maid **as a means to fight tensions**.

466. -- There is a need for the **golden mean**. *['golden mean' -- a course of action that is not extreme]*

MERCY

467. -- We do not want to survive **on anyone's mercy**.

MILE

468. -- It is inspiring to see people **going the extra mile** to help the poor. *['go the extra mile' -- to make a special effort for a particular purpose]*

MIND

469. -- That unfortunate event left **a bad feeling in his mind**.

470. -- If they do not **open their mind** to all different people, they will not find the best candidate. || It is a great way to put aside daily stress and **open your mind** to more creative ways of thinking. *['open your mind' -- to accept new ideas']*

471. -- You have **spoken out my mind**.

472. -- He has **lost his mind**.

MOMENT

473. -- He was killed on the **spur of moment**.

MONKEY

474. -- I do not want to **make a monkey of myself** by razing my million-dollar house. *['make a monkey of myself' -- to make someone look foolish]*

MOON

475. -- All successful candidates were **over the moon**. *['over the moon' -- extremely excited and happy]*

476. -- **Once in a blue moon**, something like this happens. || Some opportunities come **once in a blue moon**. || Corruption is rife, but **once in a blue moon** the people *at the top wake up* and *swing the ax*. *['once in a blue moon' -- rarely]*

477. -- He **promised** her the **moon**. *[= to promise something impossible]*

MOUNTAIN

478. -- He made a **"mountain out of what was not even a molehill"**.

479. -- Don't expect people to **move mountains** for you. *['move mountains -- to do something that is almost impossible to achieve]*

480. -- Tax department is analyzing a **mountain of data** related to demonetized currency notes that were deposited in bank accounts.

481. -- Many Universities have a **big mountain to climb.** || Our players have not been very successful on the field and they have **a big mountain to climb**.

MOUTH

482. -- Because he has a **big mouth**, he would make suggestions. || She may have a **big mouth** and say things that are really out there. || I overreact, and have a **big mouth**, and I know that. *['have a big mouth' -- too talkative]*

483. -- The news of his success spread **by word of mouth.** || Sales were being driven **by word-of-mouth** from existing customers.

484. -- It is foolish to please society with fantasies during your wedding day if you **live from hand to mouth**. || He had to **live from hand to mouth**

after the disaster which swept through his home destroying most of his items. *['live from hand to mouth' -- to have money only for your basic needs]*

MORE

485. -- According to some people, the killing of a stubborn bear was an event **more of** disciplinary action than predatory.
486. -- She had **more than human power**.
487. -- Treat him with a "**little bit more respect**".
488. -- You need to do "**even more**" to get the first rank.
489. -- We have **more or less** decided to join the meeting. || They go online **more or less** than everyone else. *['more or less' -- almost or approximately]*

MUD

490. -- We really are here to help people become closer, **not fling mud** at each other. *['fling mud' -- to criticize somebody to damage their reputation]*

English Idioms and Phrases -- N

NAIL

491. -- They have struck yet another **nail in the coffin** of non-proliferation. *['nail in the coffin' -- something that may cause a company, plan, etc. to fail]*

492. -- Real happiness — or perhaps real joy — doesn't come easily, but is **fought for tooth and nail**. *['fight for tooth and nail -- fight fiercely]*

NAME

493. -- Main issues are at an impasse: agriculture, education, employment **to name a few**. || He called out a bunch of people like John, David, Mark, and Desmond just **to name a few**.

NARROW

494. -- He had a **narrow escape** from being drowned after he got caught in the swelling waters of the river.

NECESSARY

495. -- Return and exchange is **a necessary evil** that comes alongside selling online. || When it comes to breakups, division of assets is **a necessary evil**. *['a necessary evil' -- a bad or unlikeable thing that you have to accept]*

NECK

496. -- Every farmer in our village is **neck-deep in debt**.

NEED

497. -- Online registration is **need of the hours**. || It is the **need of the hours** to protect the eyewitnesses. || The plan of having an alternate supply chain is the **need of the hours**. || A cross-section of the people says that meter fitted autos are the **need of the hours**.

NERVE
498. -- He **has got on my nerves**. || *['get on nerves' -- to annoy somebody]*
499. -- They went from being a **bundle of nerves** to playing free and easy. *['bundle of nerves' -- to be very nervous]*

NEST
500. -- The silence is much more comforting instead of **stirring up a hornet's nest**. *['a hornet's nest' -- a complicated situation in which a lot of people get very angry]*

NEEDLE
501. -- The **needle of suspicion** had initially pointed/moved towards his neighbor.

NEVER
502. -- I **never in a hundred years** thought they would do that, so we were really under shock. || **Never in a hundred years**, would I have imagined that I would be told I had cancer. || **Never in a hundred years** could I go to the moon. *['never in a hundred years' -- hardly ever]*

NOISE
503. -- I wanted to **make a noise about** things I thought were unjust. || Many organizations were set to **make a noise about** climate change last weekend. *['make a noise about something' -- to make a strong complaint about something]*

NOOSE
504. -- Investigating agency slowly and steadily **tightening the noose** around him. || Do not try to **tighten the noose** around social media. *['tighten the noose' -- to make a situation more difficult for someone]*

NOSE

505. -- Have you a right to **stick your nose** into everyone's business. *['stick your nose' -- to interfere]*

NOTE

506. -- Meeting **ended on a positive note**. || He wants to **end** his managerial tenure at the club **on a positive note**. || Stock market **closed on a positive note** for the fourth day. *['ended, closed, left, etc. on a positive note' -- something has a good ending]*

507. -- It is probably better to **strike a note of** caution. || They decided to **strike a note of** kinship with the migrants. *['strike a note of' -- to express a particular feeling about something]*

NOWHERE

508. -- You **get nowhere** without hard work/compassion. || He flailed and fought but **got nowhere**. || The whole world knew he was going to **get nowhere**.

English Idioms and Phrases -- O

OCEAN
509. -- An **ocean of opportunities/troubles** was waiting for him. || His statement drowned me in the **ocean of guilt**. || We are swimming in **an ocean of news** throughout the day. || A drop of holiness is worth more than **an ocean of genius**. || She termed him as **an ocean of knowledge**. || The biological brain is **an ocean of electromagnetic activity**.

OFF
510. -- She told **off the record** her business was going strong. *['off the record' -- unofficially]*

ONE
511. -- Black money cannot be brought back **in one stroke**. || I want to destroy the world of terrorism **in one stroke**. *['in one stroke' -- with a single immediate action]*

512. -- They launched 10 satellites **in one go**. || All the buses would have to be reorganized **in one go**. || The documents show that the entire principal amount was not paid **in one go**. *['in one go' -- at the same time]*

513. -- It is not the question of **one's victory or other's defeat**; It is a question of the welfare of the state.

514. -- There were beautiful toys; **one was superior to the other**.

515. -- We should not accept racism even if it is **one or two** or three incidents. || The government has been urged to pick **one or two** public universities to be upgraded to global status. *['one or two' -- some, a few]*

516. -- It was at the **stroke of midnight** that India got freedom.

ONCE
517. -- **Once or twice** every winter we get prolonged flooding in our region. *['once or twice' -- a few times]*

518. -- We must end gender-based violence **once and for all**. || She has now settled the debate **once and for all**. *['once and for all' -- completely or finally]*

OPEN
519. -- If I **open my mouth,** a lot of people will be in trouble.
520. -- They feared that the new law would **open floodgates for** the prosecution of citizens for minor offenses.

OPPORTUNITY
521. -- He took a vow to take revenge **at the first opportunity**.
522. -- She got a **golden opportunity** to establish his identity in the world.
523. -- They **made the most of his opportunity**.

ORDER
524. -- Selfishness is the **order of the day**.
525. -- It will take me a lot of time to **put things back in order**.
526. -- They shout their name, address, caste and age' -- **in that order**.

OVER
527. -- The issue of the effect of taxation or royalties on coal was studied **over and over again**. *[over and over again -- many times]*
528. -- A drought-affected farmer said: **'over my dead body** would I allow political leaders into my village'

English Idioms and Phrases -- P, Q

PACE
529. -- Waterlogged roads caused traffic to move at a **snail's pace** in many places.

PAINT
530. -- Police **painted the firing incident** as an encounter for self-defense.

PALM
531. -- Live in the present and appreciate all of the opportunities and great times you **have in the palm of your hand.** *['have somebody/something in the palm of your hand' -- to have complete control over somebody/something]*

PAR
532. -- President's security would be **on a par with** Prime Minister. || Toll charges on this stretch would be **on a par with** other National Highways. || Care and Protection of Children Act does not permit treating minor offenders **on a par with** adults for trial and punishment. *['on a par with' -- equal in importance or quality to]*

PARALLEL
533. -- She seemed to **draw a parallel between** riding a roller coaster and raising a child. *['draw a parallel between' -- to find similar features]*
534. -- Chief Minister released a list of candidates, **parallel to the one** issued officially by the party chief.

PART
535. -- Social media is **part and parcel** of the life we live now. || Much like football, victory and defeat are **part and parcel** of politics. || Injury is **part**

and parcel of a sportsperson's life. More so in contact sports like boxing. *['part and parcel of' -- an essential part of]*

PASS

536. -- Department officials **passed the buck** and refrained from taking action. || They **passed the buck** on junior officers. *['pass the buck' -- the act of attributing to another person or group one's own responsibility]*

PEAK

537a. -- Resentment among employees **boiled** to its **peak**.
537b. -- The enthusiasm of the students **reached** its **peak**.
538. -- He is moving towards the **peak of** her **career**.

PENNY

539. -- You will not get any help, **not a penny**. || In the seven months since the fund was launched, **not a penny** has been used. || In Israel, those who use the water cover the full cost, with **not a penny** of government subsidy. *['not a penny' -- not a little sum of money]*

PICK

540. -- He frequently **picked fights** with others. || We do not **pick** unnecessary **fights**.

PICKLE

541. -- He ran through the stop sign and got caught **in a pickle**. *['in a pickle' -- in a difficult or unpleasant situation]*

PICTURE

542. -- We are yet to **get a full picture** of the incident. || It took me three minutes to **get a full picture**. *['get a picture' -- to understand a situation]*
543. -- No one has the **full picture of the situation** on the ground.

PIECE

544. -- Accused were taken to the crime scene, **to piece together the** sequence of events. || Officials are trying **to piece together the** possible motivations of the attacker. || Police **pieced together** the narrative behind the kidnap in the industrial area.

545. -- Case soon **fell to pieces** after cops investigated the matter.

546. -- People battled hard to **pick up the pieces of** life but occasional heavy rains threatened to revive the *ghost of flooding*. || They were left to **pick up the pieces**, wondering if they will keep their jobs or ever get paid. || She is helping victims of violent crime **pick up the pieces.** *['pick up the pieces' --- to return to normal position after suffering a shock]*

PILL

547. -- Retirement before the age of 40 is a **bitter pill to swallow**. || Without a considerable salary life becomes **a bitter pill to swallow**. || A record-breaking defeat was undoubtedly a **bitter pill to swallow** for our team. *['bitter pill to swallow' -- a very unpleasant fact that you have to accept]*

PILLAR

548. -- He had to **run from pillar to post** for compensation from the power department, but to no avail. || I have been **running from pillar to post** to get a suitable post allocated. *['run from pillar to post' -- to be forced to go from one person, office, situation, etc. to another fruitlessly]*

PINCH

549. -- In tough economic times, it is often the small businesses that **feel the pinch** the most. || If we, the middle class, **feel the pinch**, it is much harder for the poor. *['feel the pinch' -- to not have enough money]*

PLACE

550. -- They should **put in place** a number of measures for speedy investigation.

PLAN
551. -- His kidnapping was said to have been **planned to perfection**.

PLAY
552. -- 11-year-old boy **played the dead**. || He often **plays the fool**. *['play the dead, fool, etc.' -- to pretend that you are dead, fool, etc.]*

553. -- Rain **played spoilsport** as three days of the play were washed out on the trot.

554. -- Some sections of the society are trying to **play up the issue** even when things are pretty much normal. *['play up' -- to try to make something seem more important than it is]*

555. -- Police officers **played old song**: 'Give proof, will act. *['played old song -- to repeat something in a boring way]*

556. -- Nobody should **play politics** on villagers' land.

557. -- The sun is **playing hide and seek**.

PLUG
558. -- The government decided to **pull the plug** on cooking gas subsidies. *['pull the plug' -- to end something]*

POINT
559. -- They have pushed us to a **point of no return**. || He described the situation as **"a point of no return"**.

560. -- We are insensitive **to the point of** inflicting cruelty on victims.

561. -- Loss and damage have continually been **a sore point** in climate change talks since first introduced around 2007. *['a sore point' -- something that may upset you whenever it is mentioned]*

562. -- My efforts were not in vain, they were just **beside the point**. *['to be beside the point' -- to distract from the main topic]*

POISON
563. -- She was believed to have **poisoned the ears** of his son against her daughter-in-law. *['poison the ears' -- to say critical things about somebody]*

POSTURE
564. -- Administration chose to maintain an **ostrich-like posture**. *[= to notice something but decide not to take any action]*

POWER
565. -- He does not want to annoy the **powers-that-be**. || The **powers-that-be** should recognize that they do not always know best. *['powers-that-be' -- used to refer to those individuals or groups who collectively hold authority at the top]*

PRETEXT
566. -- Inspector took him along **on the pretext of** interrogation. || A stranger, **on the pretext of** giving him money, diverted his attention and replaced his debit card with another. || They were imposing a hefty penalty on taxi drivers **on the pretext of** violation of rules. *['on the pretext of' -- as an excuse of]*

PRICE
567. -- We want peace **at any price**.

PRISM
568. -- Students looked at the Budget through **a prism of its own**.

PROPHET
569. -- From what I witnessed on that day, though I am not a **prophet of doom**, a major disaster is lurking around the water bodies. *['prophet of doom' -- a predictor of bad happenings]*

PROS

570. -- Do you know the **pros and cons** of social networking? || She wanted to discover the **pros and cons** of solo travel. *['pros and cons' -- advantages and disadvantages]*

PULL

571. -- I was being **pulled and pushed** in every direction.

572. -- You must know how to stand up against all **pulls and pressures** by rivals. *['pulls and pressures' -- strong resistance]*

PUNCTURE

573. -- Higher interest rates and dearer fuel have **punctured the momentum** of the car industry.

PUSH

574. -- While lead in water is a hot topic, the mayor says there is no need to **push the panic button.** *['push the panic button' -- respond to a situation by panicking or taking emergency measures.]*

QUIET

575. -- They have gone through **quite a lot** and it has been quite a long journey.

English Idioms and Phrases -- R

RACE

576. -- Rescuers were in a **race against time** to find survivors of a powerful earthquake amid forecasts of heavy rain and cold overnight. *['a race against time' -- a situation in which something must be done before a particular point in time.]*

RAGE

577. -- The hunger monkeys **fly into a rage**. || Without the medication, he can **fly into a rage**. || He **flew into a rage** and told his wife he did not want to share his house with a dog and if she did buy one he would leave. || It is learned he **flew into a rage** on tasting the food. *['fly into a rage' -- to be extremely angry]*

578. -- She immediately **went into a panic and a rage**

RAIL

579. -- Don't make excuses for things when something has **gone off the rails.**

RAIN

580a. -- **Bullet rained** at us from the front.

580b. -- The accused allegedly **rained blows** on him till he fell unconscious.

580c. -- It is **raining resignation** in the company.

581. -- The eroded roads are more apparent when it is **raining cats and dogs**. *[= raining heavily]*

RAISE

582. -- **Fingers are being raised at** the police failure in exposing the case.

583. -- A boy spotted the body in the cane field and **raised an alarm**. *['raise an alarm' -- to make a loud noise or signal to alert other people]*

584. -- Opposition members **raised a ruckus**. *['raise a ruckus' -- to create confusion]*

585. -- The ideal presidency is one that **raises the least heat and dust**.

586. -- His move has **raised more questions than answers**.

587. -- Just as I was getting accustomed to my job, the manager raised the bar and I had to perform even better *['raise the bar' -- to set a higher standard of quality, etc.]*

588. -- Here is some news that will definitely raise your eyebrows *['raise your eyebrows' -- to show your disapproval]*

RAY

589. -- Her daughter-in-law has truly brought a **ray of sunshine** into her house. || We paused for a moment to enjoy a **ray of sunshine** in an otherwise bleak time for the real estate business.

REIN

590. -- He was fortunate to find a job and an employer that allowed him to **give full rein** to it. *['give full rein to' -- to give complete freedom]*

REST

591. -- The pandemonium has almost been **put to rest**. *['put to rest' -- to dispel]*

592. -- Foreign minister **set at rest** media speculation about the terrorists-linked group.

RESULT

593. -- We are getting no support at all **as a result of which** our business is completely going down.

RAPID

594. -- Three bullets struck him **in rapid succession**. || She has released three albums **in rapid succession**.

RICH

595. -- Mike Tyson went **from rags to riches** and back again over the course of his career. || The odds of going **from rags-to-riches** here have always been fairly low. *['from rags to riches' -- from being poor or deprived to being super rich]*

ROLL

596. -- All his friends are **rolling in wealth.** || Their families are not dirt poor but they are not **rolling in wealth**, either.

ROOF

597. -- If the results are positive, the stock could **go through the roof**. || Water and electric bills **went through the roof**, *['go through the roof' -- (of prices or figures) to raise or increase quickly and unexpectedly.]*

ROOT

598. -- We are working towards reaching the **root cause** of all problems. || What is the **root cause** of terror attacks?

ROSY

599. -- His **medical report is not rosy** as of now, with the next 24 to 48 hours being extremely critical for him.

ROUND

600. -- A few names for the post are **doing rounds.** || There are a couple of theories **doing the rounds.** *['do rounds' -- to pass on quickly from one person to another person]*

601. -- We learn lessons in a **roundabout manner.**

RUB

602. -- We would not like to **rub salt on his wounds.** *['rub salt on wounds' -- to make a bad experience even worse for somebody]*

RUN

603. -- He is still **in the running** for a global award worth one million dollars.

604. -- Though there were challenges with the online learner application system, it is now **up and running.** *['up and running' -- working effectively or efficiently]*

RUNG

605. -- She climbed several **rungs of the corporate ladder.**

English Idioms and Phrases -- S

SAME

606. -- My new job is **much the same** as the old one. || Result remained **much the same** in the second game.

607. -- Party leaders seemed to be **milking the same old cows** of community, caste and convenience.

608. -- We are **on the same page** on a range of issues. *['on the same page' -- having similar thoughts]*

SAVE

609. -- A good rule for wise financial management is to **save something for a rainy day**. *['save something for a rainy day' -- to save something for a time when you may need it unexpectedly]*

SAY

610. -- DCP refused to disclose findings, **except to say** the accused was not fit enough.

611. -- His behavior is disturbing, **to say the least**.

612. -- **Needless to say** that he will not join our company. *['needless to say' -- you already know or would expect)]*

SCENE

613. -- Protestors **created quite a scene**.

SCRATCH

614. -- We do not want to start **from scratch**. *['from scratch' -- from the very beginning]*

615. -- Never mind that the award has left people across the world **scratching their heads**. || He likes writing columns for the paper, even if they make you **scratch your head** sometimes. *['scratch your heads' -- to think hard to find an answer to something]*

SEAT

616. -- Youth are now more practical, emotions may have **taken a back seat**. *['take a back seat' -- not to play an important role in something]*

SEED

617. -- His strange behavior **planted seeds of doubt** in the mind of the police.

618. -- If anyone wants to **sow seeds of division** among us, we will not let that happen.

619. -- In their **hunger for power,** some people tried to **sow the seeds of casteism.**

SECOND

620. -- As a singer, he is **second to none.** *['second to none' -- best]*

SEE

621. -- Critical comments from his rivals made him **see red**. || Gambling operators **see red** over the prohibition on card games. *['see red' -- to be extremely angry]*

SEEP

622. -- A lot of **awareness is seeping** into the rural regions.

SET

623. -- It is up to the teachers to **set things right.**

SETTLE

624. -- I took a vow to **settle** the **score** with them one day. || Supporters of different parties tried to **settle** the **score** after the election. || They had a "personal grudge" against him and they wanted to **settle an old score** with him. *['settle the score' -- to take revenge]*

SHADOW

625. -- The **shadow of apprehensions** appears to loom over the meeting once again.

626. -- He lives **under the shadow of death.** || The elections were held **under the shadow of** the **attacks**. || They have lived their whole lives **under the shadow of war**.

627. -- She has **risen from the shadows**.

SHAKE

628. -- He replied with a **shaking voice**. || From her **shaking voice** and stumbling words, she sounds really scared and intimidated. || A boy with a **shaking voice** made the distress call from a sinking ferry.

629. -- Their act was sufficient to **shake the soul** of our nation.

SHAPE

630. -- Army men faced 'disciplinary action' **in the shape of a** court-martial.

SHELL

631. -- You need to **come out of your shell** and show the world what a fun-loving person you are. *['come out of your shell' -- to become more comfortable and friendly with people]*

SHOCK

632. -- He **got the shock of his life** when he found that an amount of dollar 1 million was debited from his account through a bogus check. *['get the shock of the life' -- to suffer the biggest blow in the life]*

SHOOT

633. -- He was **shooting his mouth off** about Canada **being** a future champion and the rival **being** past of its prime.

634a. -- He **shot into the limelight** on Nov 12, 2014.

634b. -- She **shot into statewide fame** soon.

634c. -- They **shot into the glare of the media**.

SHOULDER

635. -- It is difficult for any particular politician to **stand head and shoulders** above the crowd.

636. -- Let us walk **shoulder to shoulder** and do some good work for the nation. *['shoulder to shoulder' -- as one group with the same aims]*

SHOW

637. -- Festival was celebrated with great **pomp and show**.

638. -- Party workers walked into the city for the **show of strength**.

SHOWER

639. -- We cannot talk peace **under a shower of bullets**.

SIDE

640. -- He is on the **right side of forty**. *[= below 40 years of age]*

641. -- Students have made both online and over the counter, submissions **to be on the safe side**.

642. -- We do not want to **get on the wrong side of the** judiciary. || Those found **on the wrong side of the** law should face criminal prosecution. *['on the wrong side of the law, judiciary, etc.' -- having to deal with police, court, etc, because they have been part of an illegal activity]*

SIGH

643. -- Principal's order led to a **collective sigh of relief.** || Entire region seemed to **breathe a sigh of relief** that the worst was over. || People are **breathing a sigh of relief** with the opening of the city control center. || They **breathed a collective sigh of relief** when their family members were released from jail.

SING

644. -- Today, he **sang a different tune**. *['sing a different tune' -- to behave in a different way]*

SINK

645. -- Battered by scams, his **ship is sinking**.

646a. -- Doping scandal **sank his career**.

646b. -- Her reputation **sunk to a new low**.

SIX

647. -- Both the patient and care manager were at **sixes and sevens** not knowing what to do. || Syria was in **sixes and sevens** and Syrians were scattered across borders. *['sixes and sevens' -- state of great confusion and disagreement]*

SKY

648. -- The rent rates **reached the sky**.

649. -- I **praised** him **to the skies**.

650. -- One defeat does not mean the **sky is falling**.

651. -- Wails of protestors **rent the sky**. || Guns fired the last salute and the cannon **rent the sky**.

SLATE

652. -- They all wanted to **start with a clean slate** in a completely new environment. *['start with a clean slate' -- to start afresh]*

SLEEP

653. -- Higher authorities **were "sleeping"**. *[= not taking any action]*

654. -- Officials have been **losing sleep**. || This issue is really worrying and I am **losing sleep** over it. || He was **losing sleep** because he was convinced there was a lion in his garden. *['lose sleep -- to be very tense]*

655. -- What has **robbed** several hundred people in these villages **of** their **sleep**?

SLIDE
656a. -- She was **sliding into depression**.
656b. -- They have been **sliding into** their **old ways**.

SLOPE
657. -- The right to die may put us on a very **slippery slope.**

SLUMBER
658. -- Serial blasts jolted the government **out of its deep slumber**.

SMACK
659. -- His actions **smack of** a vendetta. || Her statement **smacked of** a delusion of grandeur and disregard for the law. *['smack of something' – to involve a particular unpleasant quality]*

SMELL
660. -- The sequence of happenings emitted the **smell of a conspiracy**. | We got the **smell of tension**.
661. -- They **smelled trouble** when a woman tried to get a cell phone and presented a fake ID.
662. -- When something sounds too good to be true, I usually **smell a rat**. *['smell a rat' -- to be suspicious]*

SMILE
663a. -- **Life** was **smiling** upon her once more.
663b. -- At last, **fortune smiled** on him.
663c. -- His **luck smiled** on him on Jan 25.
663d. -- I see the moon **smiling down** at me.

SNAIL
664. -- Traffic on this stretch **moves at a snail's pace**. *[= to be very slow]*

SOUND
665. -- **Strange it may sound**, but the truth is that many villagers who have contracted dengue are unaware of the fact that it is caused by mosquitoes. || Turning e-waste into income is no longer an impossible feat, however **strange it may sound** at first.

SOURCE
666. -- Nigel, **going by sources,** was known to all his neighbors.

SPADE
667. -- **Call a spade a spade** and **criticism will rain** on you. *['call a spade a spade' -- to say exactly what you think without trying to hide your opinion]*

SPAN
668. -- Certain essential oils that have antimicrobial properties can help you get your entire home **spic and span** in a natural, chemical-free way. *['spic and span' -- neat and clean]*

SPARE
669. -- We will **not spare the efforts** from our side.

SPARK
670. -- Many players fall short after **showing initial spark**.

SPATE
671. -- After the deluge in northern and coastal regions, rivers in the southern districts were **in full spate**.

SPEAK

672. -- The **facts speak** clearly to the irrelevance of many policies.

SPEECH

673. -- He gave a **flowery speech** about leading the fight against illiteracy. *['flowery speech' -- full of lovely words but without substance]*

SPILL

674. -- **Pain and anger spilled** onto the streets.

675. -- She was eager to finally **spill the beans** on her husband's lifestyle. *['spill the beans' -- to tell the secret]*

SPIN

676. -- His **world began spinning** after he lost his job. *[= to be extremely worried and desperate]*

SPIRAL

677. -- I am appalled at how things are **spiraling out of control**.

SPOT

678. -- Some airports do not have a **spotless record** when it comes to scrutiny over security arrangements.

SQUARE

679. -- Now I am **square up with** you. *['square up with' -- to pay money that you owe]*

680. -- The situation **got back to square one** after some time. *['got back to square one' -- returned to original state without making any progress]*

STAB

681. -- She says that the **stab in the back** may come anytime, anywhere. *['stab in the back' -- a betrayal by your friend, close relative, etc.]*

STAIN
682. -- You should be proud that I don't have a **stain of corruption** on me.

STAND
683. -- They **stood firmly with** the people of their neighboring country in the hour of grief and prayed for normalcy to return soon.

684. -- You need to learn how to fight and **stand on your own feet**. *['stand on your own feet' -- to be independent and able to take care of yourself]*

STAY
685. -- It is a battle just to **stay afloat**. *[stay afloat -- able to survive]*

STEAM
686. -- This **issue has lost steam.** *[= no longer effective]*

687. -- Ceasefire efforts **gathered steam.** *[= getting effective]*

STOCK
688. -- The pharmacy inside the hospital is often **out of stock**.

STONE
689. -- It is a **huge stone off my chest**.

690. -- They are **leaving no stone unturned** to help their candidates win the maximum possible votes. || His detractors have **left no stone unturned** to defame him.

691. -- Self-belief is the **stepping stone** to success.

692. -- He sat in **stony silence**.

STORM
693. -- His words against the doctor **created a storm.**

694. -- She went to the premiere to experience **the calm before the storm**. *['the calm before the storm' -- a calm time before a possible violent activity]*

695. -- He has **lit stuttering oil lamps in the midst of storms.**

696. -- She found herself **in a storm** for her controversial remark.

STRAIGHT

697 -- They are **heading straight to hell**.

698. -- Orders are coming **straight from the top**.

699. -- Ask him about his favorite role and he says he wants to play **straight and simple** characters.

STRAW

700. -- The rise of the currency proved to be **the last straw** for its economy. *['last straw' -- the last in a series of unpleasant events that makes the situation go beyond control]*

STRONG

701. -- Our campaign will **go strong** in the coming days. || We can still **go strong** despite all the problems.

SWEAR

702. -- She always **swears by** New York. || In courts, many people **swear by** the constitution instead of religious books.

SWEEP

703. -- Similar **speculation has swept** across the cities.

SWEET

704. -- He gave me some **sweet news**.

English Idioms and Phrases -- T

TABLE

705. -- You do not always know what they will **bring to the table** on the given day. *['bring to the table' -- to contribute something useful to a debate, plan, etc.]*

706. -- It is only a matter of time before the **tables are turned** before the tide is reversed, and the winner is on the losing side. *['turn the tables' -- to completely reverse the situation]*

TAKE

707. -- Adverse weather **took a heavy toll** on his health. || Growing pile of stressed loans **took a heavy toll** on banks' health. *['take a heavy toll' -- to have bad effects]*

708. -- Guilty cops will be **taken to task**. *['take to task' -- to severely criticize]*

709. -- His credibility has **taken a nosedive**. *['take a nosedive' -- to worsen]*

710. -- We should applaud that sort of sincere journalism which does not try to **take sides**, but merely presents the facts on the ground. || She does not **take sides** and instead tries to understand all perspectives.

711. -- You are **taking things too far**. *[= taking a minor argument, etc. seriously.]*

712. -- It **takes ages** to build a reputation.

713. -- It will take a long time for things **to take a place**.

714. -- Sugar production **took a hit** last year.

715. -- I **take pains** to maintain a healthy lifestyle. || He had to **take pains** to reach there for administrative help.

716. -- Most of us **take for granted** the roofs we have over our heads. || 'Law enforcement' is a profession many **take for granted** but few have the dedication and calling to pursue. *['take for granted' -- to not recognize the real value of something]*

717. -- Education **takes up the lion's share** of childcare expenses.
718. -- His image has **taken a huge beating**.

TALK

719. -- Her in-laws were not **on talking terms** with her. || Many people who co-founded companies together are now not **on talking terms**.
720. -- **Talks have not frozen** between the two countries.
721. -- His holiday party is the **talk of the town**.

TASTE

722. -- His comments were criticized for being **in 'poor taste'**.

TEAR -1

723. -- Many students stood for several minutes to clap and shout their joy, with some **shedding tears of relief**.
724. -- He appeared **close to tears**.
725. -- Arrival of rescue teams left survivors **shedding tears of joy**.

TEAR -2

726. -- We do not want his body **torn to bits**.

TEMPEST

727. -- Ban on free books over corporate logo was like **a tempest in a teapot**. *['a tempest in a teapot' -- extreme worry about an unimportant thing]*

TERM

728. -- Don't view the problem of terrorism **in terms of** political benefit or loss.
729. -- I have lived the world **on my own terms**. || She sings **on her own terms**.

TENTACLE

730. -- The **tentacles of the scam** went up to the offices of the governor. || His loyalists have actually got embroiled in **the tentacles of the law**.|| The police will now interrogate them to trace **the tentacles of the espionage network**.

THICK

731. -- Allegations **flew thick and fast** in the administration. *['thick and fast' -- one after another; quickly]*

732. -- Best friendships are between people who share the same value system, stick with each other **through thick and thin.** || I am overwhelmed by the way in which my fans have stood by me **through thick and thin.** *['through thick and thin' -- in both good and bad situations]*

733. -- One needs to be a little **thick**-**skinned** when one wants to be on social networking sites. *['thick skinned' -- not affected by the criticism]*

THINK

734. -- He is starting to **think big**.

735. -- You must **think twice** before investing your money in mutual funds. *['think twice' -- to think carefully before taking a decision on something]*

736. -- The people **thought highly of** him.

737. -- A soldier used his **smart thinking** to trap the enemy.

THROW

738. -- The station is **within a stone's throw** from my village. *['a stone's throw' -- very short distance]*

739. -- People install boards and plates mentioning their designation on their vehicles with an intention to **throw their weight around.**

TIGER

740. -- There is a **tiger inside me.**

TIME

741. -- Company **ran out of time** to train its newly-recruited staff.

742. -- Education policy has remained **out of step with the time**.

743. -- I love the company of her **all the time**.

744. -- Robbers slapped him a **couple of times**.

745. -- She is considered one of the best woman authors **of all time**.

746. -- We are **behind the times** and that is not a position we want to be in.

747. -- **Time** is not an effective **healer for** some **wounds**.

748. -- I have seen **hard times**.

749. -- They had met in person only a **handful of times**.

TIP

750. -- This is **just the tip of the iceberg**. *['the tip of the iceberg' -- only a small part of a much larger problem]*

TOE

751. -- Health department was **on the toes** with a sudden spurt in a number of suspected chickenpox cases in the district. *['on the toes' -- very alert]*

TOUCH

752. -- Prices of various pulses and vegetables are already **touching the sky**.

753. -- They are **too politically important to touch**.

TONGUE

754. -- Some employees have **a loose tongue** when it comes to sharing company information on the web.

TOP

755. -- It is one thing to **get to the top** and it is another to stay there.

756. -- Here are a few that **went over the top**. *['over the top' -- done exaggeratedly and with too much effort]*

757. -- Our team members were **on top of the world** as we won the world cup final. *['on top of the world' -- very happy or proud]*

TOSS
758. -- I kept **tossing** and **turning** at night.

759. -- The entire process **has gone for a toss**.

TRADE
760. -- He is a blacksmith **by trade**.

TREAD
761. -- She does not believe in **treading a beaten path**. *['tread a beaten path' -- to follow a general way of life]*

TREATMENT
762. -- He accused the center of meting out **'step-motherly' treatment** to the state.

TUNE
763. -- Scam relating to excavation and illegal quarrying was **to the tune of** several million. || Investigation agency has registered a case against a private company for allegedly cheating a bank to the tune of dollar 100 million. *['to the tune of' -- involving too much cost]*

TURN
764. -- She screamed at him, **turned purple with rage** and threw a satellite dish near him.

765. -- It was an important opportunity to **turn over a new leaf** and hopefully build a new conversation. *['turn over a new leaf' -- to improve your personality]*

766. -- His trial saw many **twists and turns**.

767. -- **Turn the screws** on the regime.

768. -- The bad have nowhere to hide in a working system and the **good may turn bad** when in a rotten system.

769. -- Opposition parties have **turned on the heat** on the ruling party in the House.

770. -- There is **no silver bullet to turn things** around immediately.

TWILIGHT

771. -- Elder people should not be permitted to be left unattended **in the twilight of their lives**.

TWIST

772. -- I am surprised at the way **things are twisted** out of proportion.

English Idioms and Phrases -- U, V

UNDER

773. -- If this is the state of affairs right **under the nose of the government** in the capital, one can easily understand the situation in remote areas. || She **stole her show from under President's nose.** || Attackers managed to flee from **under the noses of the cops.** || Agitators ransacked the office **right under the nose of the police.** *['under the nose of' -- in the presence of]*

774. -- Nothing will be **brushed under the carpet.** || The taboo surrounding mental illnesses is largely responsible for the issue of depression being **brushed under the carpet** umpteen times. *['brush under the carpet' -- to hide a problem or try to keep it secret]*

VEIN

775. -- She told him in **a lighter vein**, 'when you are busy, I am not visible at all!'. || He has dealt with the serious issue **in a lighter vein** in his film. || A reply would be made **in the same vein.** *['in a…vein' -- in a particular style]*

VERGE

776. -- He was **on the verge of** drowning in quicksand on the river banks. || He was **on the verge of** losing cool. *['on the verge of' -- near to the moment when something takes place]*

VOICE

777a. -- Senior leaders have been **speaking in different voices** on this issue.

777b. -- "Caged parrot" speaks **in** its **master voice.**

VOID

778. -- In case any winner refuses to accept the prize, his/her participation in the contest will be declared **null and void.** || Lieutenant Governor declared the order **"null and void"**, saying the chief minister did not seek his prior approval. [*'null and void' -- no longer valid*]

VOW

779a. -- He continued to abide by his original **vow of allegiance.** [= *promise to be loyal*]

779b. -- He fulfilled his **vow of vengeance** against his enemy three months later at his home. [= *swear to take revenge*]

English Idioms and Phrases -- W-Z

WAKE
780. -- Pressure mounted on him to quit **in the wake of** the scandal. || Many cities beefed up their security **in the wake of** the horrific terror attacks. || He had to announce his resignation **in the wake of** widespread criticisms of his administration's handling of violence on campus. *['in the wake of somebody/something' -- following somebody/something]*

WALK
781a. -- The convicted juvenile **walked free** after serving his sentence.
781b. -- A 30-year-old man **walked to freedom** after the High Court acquitted him of murder.
782. -- They can now **walk tall** as a bank with ultra-modern banking technology. || She wanted to be that woman who can **walk tall**. *['walk tall' -- to feel proud or confident]*

WAR
783. -- A **war of words** erupted between two ladies. || Two organizations were embroiled in a **bitter war of words**. || There was a **war of words** in Parliament as corruption debate took center stage. || Two states are **locked in a war of words**. *['a war of words' -- strong and bitter argument/disagreement]*
784. -- Pedestrians are **on the warpath** against wrong-way riders. || Residents were **on the warpath** against official apathy in suburbs. *['be on the warpath' -- eager to fight somebody]*
785. -- A **war of sorts** erupted between two social network companies.

WAVE
786. -- 9/11 strike **sent shock waves** across the globe.
787. -- I saw a **wave of people** running. || Authorities must put an end to **a wave of vicious and violent attacks** on human rights defenders.

WAY

788. -- They accused him of feigning illness **as a way** to avoid prison.

789. -- He always **stands in my way.** || Her family let her follow her dreams and allow nothing to **stand in her way.** *['stand in the way' -- to create hurdles]*

790. -- He has his **own way in everything.**

791. -- If we win as we expect, the kind of reactions that we will take will be different if the outcome goes **the other way round.** || We need to make sure that politicians serve the people and not **the other way round.**

792. -- If you are still an uneasy shopper, **take the easy way out.**

793. -- Technology has come **a big way** into cardiology. *['in a big way' -- on a large scale]*

794. -- Residents were being forced to leave the town while the authorities continued to **look the other way.** *['look the other way' -- to intentionally avoid noticing something]*

795. -- A lot of our players are still young and have a **long way to go.**

796. -- If you **have a way with** words, writing is another job you can do from the comfort of your home, *['have a way with somebody/something' -- to be good at dealing with somebody/something]*

797. -- It is very important for an individual to manage their emotions and not **give way** to it.

798. -- They can go **out of the way** to harm him. || Strangers have **gone out of their way** to support us.

799. -- After several protests and as many assurances, nothing but disappointment **came their way.**

800. -- People at the administrative level must find **ways and means** of dealing with the problem of citizens.

WEAR
801. -- We don't have to **wear patriotism on our sleeves.**

WEB
802. -- We were stunned by his **web of lies.** || **Web of deceit** and deception was being woven by the fraudster.

WEIGH

803. -- It is important to **weigh your words** according to the compliments and express them with the best-suited vocabulary. *['weigh your words' -- to say something very carefully]*

WEIGHT

804. -- I am touched by the **weight of the responsibility** that the people of the country have put on my shoulders.

805. -- Some others are **putting** their **weight** behind him. *['put your weight behind somebody'-- to fully support somebody]*

WELCOME

806. -- He returned to a **roaring welcome** by his family members.

WELL

807. -- This cloth **will do well** for curtains.

WHEEL

808. -- We must expedite the **wheel of justice.**

809. -- **Keep the wheels of progress turning** smoothly.

810. -- There are **wheels within wheels** in the defense ministry. *['wheels within wheels' -- incomprehensible situation because it involves complicated and secret processes]*

811. -- I am optimistic that the **wheel of fortune** would turn in favor of us in the future.

WHOLE

812. -- Flag shall be destroyed **as a whole** in a private. || Arrest of an army officer cannot be regarded as a taint on the military **as a whole**. || If a legislative decision impacts society **as a whole**, how can someone claim this is a women's only issue?

WIND

813. -- He can run **like the wind** and not get tired. *['like the wind' -- very fast]*

814. -- **Throwing all the rules to the winds**, a guard allowed his relatives to enter into the control room.

815. -- I have **got wind of your moves** a few days ago itself.

WIPE

816. -- Do you know the city that rebels have repeatedly threatened to **wipe off the map**? *['wipe off the map' -- to destroy completely]*

WIRE

817. -- World cup final witnessed a high-voltage contest that **went down to the wire**. *[=result was not decided until the very end]*

WIT

818. -- It appears he is **off his wits**. || He chooses to live **off his wits**, and trust his luck and fate. *['off his wits' -- unable to think clearly]*

WOOD

819. -- Performance review of the offices is conducted to **weed out deadwood**.

WORD

820. -- Militants should be condemned in the **strongest words**.

821a. -- He was **at a loss of words** to explain what went wrong. || I was **lost for words.**

821b. -- We are **short of words**. || She seems to be **falling short of words** to describe his pretty daughter. || She was **falling short of words** while expressing her feelings. || He **fell short of words** to describe his memories.

822. -- I have **given him the word**. *[= to promise]*

823. -- There were **no words left** to express dismay.

824. -- They **exchanged hot words** in a debate over water shortage.

825. -- I **don't have a good word to say** about a person involved in illegal activities.

826. -- They used posters and flyers to **spread the word around**.

827. -- **Word soon spread** in the village.

828. -- Finally, she had to **eat her words**. *['eat your words' -- to accept what you said was wrong]*

829. -- His **words** are in **everyone's mouth**.

830. -- His doctor's **words worked magic.**

WORM

831. -- His statement on reservation policy has **opened** a fresh **can of worms**. || A parliamentary bill had security officials concerned that it would **open up a can of worms** for the prosecution of officials. *['open up a can of worms' -- to start doing something that creates a lot of difficult problems]*

WRIT

832. -- Feeling of helplessness is **writ large** on the faces of villagers. *['writ large' – easy to see]*

YEAR

833. -- We are in our **sunset years**.

YES

834. -- We cannot rely on him anymore as he has proven to be only a **"yes man"** to the management.

YOUNG

835. -- His mother and mother-in-law are **young at heart**. *['young at heart' -- to behave like a young person]*

****

About the Author

Manik Joshi was born on January 26, 1979, at Ranikhet, a picturesque town in the Kumaon region of the Indian state of Uttarakhand. He is a permanent resident of the Sheeshmahal area of Kathgodam located in the city of Haldwani in the Kumaon region of Uttarakhand in India. He completed his schooling in four different schools. He is a science graduate in the ZBC – zoology, botany, and chemistry – subjects. He is also an MBA with a specialization in marketing. Additionally, he holds diplomas in "computer applications", "multimedia and web-designing", and "computer hardware and networking". During his schooldays, he wanted to enter the field of medical science; however, after graduation, he shifted his focus to the field of management. After obtaining his MBA, he enrolled in a computer education center; he became so fascinated with working on the computer that he decided to develop his career in this field. Over the following years, he worked at some computer-related full-time jobs. Following that, he became interested in Internet Marketing, particularly in domaining (business of buying and selling domain names), web design (creating websites), and various other online jobs. However, later he shifted his focus solely to self-publishing. Manik is a nature-lover. He has always been fascinated by overcast skies. He is passionate about traveling and enjoys solo travel most of the time rather than traveling in groups. He is actually quite a loner who prefers to do his own thing. He likes to listen to music, particularly when he is working on the computer. Reading and writing are definitely his favorite pastimes, but he has no interest in sports. Manik has always dreamed of a prosperous life and prefers to live a life of luxury. He has a keen interest in politics because he believes it is politics that decides everything else. He feels a sense of gratification sharing his experiences and knowledge with the outside world. However, he is an introvert by nature and thus gives prominence to only a few people in his personal life. He is not a spiritual man, yet he actively seeks knowledge about the metaphysical world; he is particularly interested in learning about life beyond death. In addition to writing academic/informational text and fictional content, he also maintains a personal diary. He has always had a desire to stand out from the crowd. He does not believe in treading the beaten path and avoids copying someone else's path to success. Two things he always refrains from are smoking and drinking; he is a teetotaler and very health-conscious. He usually wakes up before the sun rises. He starts his morning with meditation and exercise. Fitness is an integral and indispensable part of his life. He gets energized by solving complex problems. He loves himself the way he is and he loves the way he looks. He doesn't believe in following fashion trends. He dresses according to what suits him & what he is comfortable in. He believes in taking calculated risks. His philosophy is to expect the best but prepare for the worst. According to him, you can't succeed if you are unwilling to fail. For Manik, life is about learning from mistakes and figuring out how to move forward.

Amazon Author Page of Manik Joshi:
https://www.amazon.com/author/manikjoshi
Email: manik85joshi@gmail.com

BIBLIOGRAPHY

(A). SERIES TITLE: "ENGLISH DAILY USE" *[40 BOOKS]*

01. How to Start a Sentence
02. English Interrogative Sentences
03. English Imperative Sentences
04. Negative Forms In English
05. Learn English Exclamations
06. English Causative Sentences
07. English Conditional Sentences
08. Creating Long Sentences In English
09. How to Use Numbers In Conversation
10. Making Comparisons In English
11. Examples of English Correlatives
12. Interchange of Active and Passive Voice
13. Repetition of Words
14. Remarks In the English Language
15. Using Tenses In English
16. English Grammar- Am, Is, Are, Was, Were
17. English Grammar- Do, Does, Did
18. English Grammar- Have, Has, Had
19. English Grammar- Be and Have
20. English Modal Auxiliary Verbs
21. Direct and Indirect Speech
22. Get- Popular English Verb
23. Ending Sentences with Prepositions
24. Popular Sentences In English
25. Common English Sentences
26. Daily Use English Sentences
27. Speak English Sentences Every Day
28. Popular English Idioms and Phrases
29. Common English Phrases
30. Daily English- Important Notes
31. Collocations In the English Language
32. Words That Act as Multiple Parts of Speech (Part 1)
33. Words That Act as Multiple Parts of Speech (Part 2)
34. Nouns In the English Language
35. Regular and Irregular Verbs
36. Transitive and Intransitive Verbs

37. 10,000 Useful Adjectives In English
38. 4,000 Useful Adverbs In English
39. 20 Categories of Transitional Expressions
40. How to End a Sentence

****

(B). SERIES TITLE: "ENGLISH WORD POWER" *[30 BOOKS]*

01. Dictionary of English Synonyms
02. Dictionary of English Antonyms
03. Homonyms, Homophones and Homographs
04. Dictionary of English Capitonyms
05. Dictionary of Prefixes and Suffixes
06. Dictionary of Combining Forms
07. Dictionary of Literary Words
08. Dictionary of Old-fashioned Words
09. Dictionary of Humorous Words
10. Compound Words In English
11. Dictionary of Informal Words
12. Dictionary of Category Words
13. Dictionary of One-word Substitution
14. Hypernyms and Hyponyms
15. Holonyms and Meronyms
16. Oronym Words In English
17. Dictionary of Root Words
18. Dictionary of English Idioms
19. Dictionary of Phrasal Verbs
20. Dictionary of Difficult Words
21. Dictionary of Verbs
22. Dictionary of Adjectives
23. Dictionary of Adverbs
24. Dictionary of Formal Words
25. Dictionary of Technical Words
26. Dictionary of Foreign Words
27. Dictionary of Approving & Disapproving Words
28. Dictionary of Slang Words
29. Advanced English Phrases
30. Words In the English Language

****

(C). SERIES TITLE: "WORDS IN COMMON USAGE" *[10 BOOKS]*

01. How to Use the Word "Break" In English
02. How to Use the Word "Come" In English
03. How to Use the Word "Go" In English
04. How to Use the Word "Have" In English
05. How to Use the Word "Make" In English
06. How to Use the Word "Put" In English
07. How to Use the Word "Run" In English
08. How to Use the Word "Set" In English
09. How to Use the Word "Take" In English
10. How to Use the Word "Turn" In English

****

(D). SERIES TITLE: "WORDS BY NUMBER OF LETTERS" *[10 BOOKS]*

01. Dictionary of 4-Letter Words
02. Dictionary of 5-Letter Words
03. Dictionary of 6-Letter Words
04. Dictionary of 7-Letter Words
05. Dictionary of 8-Letter Words
06. Dictionary of 9-Letter Words
07. Dictionary of 10-Letter Words
08. Dictionary of 11-Letter Words
09. Dictionary of 12- to 14-Letter Words
10. Dictionary of 15- to 18-Letter Words

****

(E). SERIES TITLE: "ENGLISH WORKSHEETS" *[10 BOOKS]*

01. English Word Exercises (Part 1)
02. English Word Exercises (Part 2)
03. English Word Exercises (Part 3)
04. English Sentence Exercises (Part 1)
05. English Sentence Exercises (Part 2)
06. English Sentence Exercises (Part 3)
07. Test Your English
08. Match the Two Parts of the Words
09. Letter-Order In Words
10. Choose the Correct Spelling

Printed in Great Britain
by Amazon